Acknowledgements

I HAVE thoroughly enjoyed writing this book; and this is due in no small part to the warmth and friendliness of the people who live and work in Quarrier's Village. Everybody, from cottage parents to office staff and in all the different parts of the village, has been kind and enthusiastic and given me every assistance in the writing of the book.

In particular, I should like to thank Dr. James Minto, the General Director; Mr. John Porteous who, as unofficial Information Officer, has helped me enormously; Judy Cochrane, Education Liaison Officer; Mr. William Dunbar, Assistant Director of Child Care; and Margaret Thomson, Social Worker at the Epilepsy Centre.

There are many others I wish to thank; Viscount Muirshiel; Mr. Joseph Mortimer, Deputy General Director; Dr. John Laidlaw, Chief Consultant at the Epilepsy Centre and Mrs. Mary Laidlaw, Rehabilitation Adviser; Mr. Alf Craigmile, Social Work Manager; Mrs. Jean Morris, Clinical Psychologist; Liz Edwards, Youth and Community Worker; Martie and George Bowie and Pearl and Jonathan Bridgeman Williams; the staff of the Mitchell Library Glasgow Room; Mary Brennan who gave me access to her own research on the Canadian end of Quarrier's; Alice Blair, Secretary of Quarrier's Former Boys' and Girls' Association; Mr. Michael Laxton of the Scottish Office; and Mr. Fred Edwards, Director of Social Work in Strathclyde.

Finally, I should like to thank most sincerely the many, many Old Girls and Boys all over Britain and Canada who have shared their memories of Quarrier's with me, happy and sad; their stories have made writing this book a marvellous experience.

May, 1984

Illustrations

Page 2 taken from Swan's *Beauties of the Clyde* (Greenock Central Library)

Pages 9, 12, 17 and 20 taken from Annan's *Closes of Glasgow, 1868-1877* (Mitchell Library)

Page 52 facing, taken from Barnardo Photographic Archive

Page 75 taken from *The Home Children,* published by Watson & Dwyer Publishing Ltd., and reproduced by kind permission from the Public Archives Canada/PA-117285

All other sources for illustrations are given in the captions

THE VILLAGE

William Quarrier

THE VILLAGE

A History of Quarrier's

by

ANNA MAGNUSSON

1984

Published by

QUARRIER'S HOMES

BRIDGE OF WEIR - SCOTLAND

First Published, 1984

ISBN 0 9510044 2 5

Cover by: Bill Turnbull

Photoset in 11-point Linotype Plantin
Made and printed in Great Britain by
BEITH PRINTING CO., LTD.,
Hillington, Glasgow

Contents

For Mum, Dad and Anna

Foreword

by MAGNUS MAGNUSSON

THIS IS THE STORY of a village, a very special village—a village that stands some 16 miles from the centre of Glasgow in the rolling fields of Renfrewshire at Bridge of Weir. It is the story of a village that has been growing up for more than a century now: first, its birth as an infant hamlet in 1878 dedicated to the task of rescuing hundreds and thousands of abandoned and orphaned children from the teeming squalor of Glasgow's back-streets; then its lusty youth as what the old *North British Daily Mail* once called a full-blooded "Children's City"; and now its evolution into maturity as a true Community of Caring—for all.

This is the story of Quarrier's Village.

I suppose the easiest way to label Quarrier's is to say that it is a sort of Scottish "Barnardo Homes", and this would not be inappropriate. William Quarrier and Thomas Barnardo were more or less contemporary; they both launched their pioneering salvage work in the East Ends of their cities (Glasgow and London) in the 1860s; both expanded their work into creating custom-built Children's Homes; both men were driven by an ardent passion for practical philanthropy, a blazing desire to help deprived and hapless children. But there is one significant difference: while Barnardo's rely on sophisticated advertising techniques to raise funds, Quarrier's have never made a public appeal for money—relying, doggedly, on manna from heaven instead. And this is perhaps why *Chambers Biographical Dictionary* carries an entry for Thomas Barnardo, but none for William Quarrier.

William Quarrier was an archetypal product of the Victorian Age: born into straitened circumstances, brought up in grinding poverty, fostered on religion and nourished by the Victorian ideals of self-help and pride in position. But in Quarrier's case, the Victorian sense of righteousness never ossified into self-righteousness; he never preached what he didn't practice. After he had "made good" as a businessman in Glasgow (pulling himself up by the boot-straps to start a chain of shoe-shops), his own success never blinded him to the desperate needs of others, and with evangelical fervour he started a revolution in social attitudes towards the underprivileged—a continuing revolution to which he devoted all the rest of his life.

Foreword

In this modern age of vast Social Work departments and child-care schemes, it isn't easy to imagine the horrors of a deprived childhood in industrial cities a hundred years ago; nor is it easy to conceive of the courage, the audacity even, of Quarrier's enterprise, his single-minded determination to give homeless children, for the first time in their lives, a home.

Ah, but what is a home? The Victorians tended to sentimentalise the idea of home, just as they tended to romanticise the idea of childhood itself. Home, Sweet Home! Home is where the heart is! What is home without a mother? As John Masefield was to write in an over-quoted passage in his poem *The Everlasting Memory:*

> And he who gives a child a treat,
> Makes joy-bells ring in Heaven's street,
> And he who gives a child a home
> Builds palaces in Kingdom come.

It took a man like William Quarrier to make a "home" a practical reality for thousands of homeless children. Quarrier wanted to get away from the institutional care of children, the vast impersonal halls and dormitories of the Poorhouse; instead he conceived, built and personally ran a growing complex of cottage homes at Bridge of Weir, with house-mothers and house-fathers in charge of small groups of children: families, not inmates.

Not content with that, he plunged energetically into pioneering emigration schemes designed to give "his" children a new life and a new future in the New World, in Canada. He pioneered free sanatoria at Bridge of Weir for the treatment of that terrible scourge of yesteryear, tuberculosis. He built a Colony for the treatment of epileptics which offered sanctuary to the victims of the "falling disease" long before it was properly understood—and all in a spirit of what he himself described as "sanctified common sense".

Over the decades since Quarrier built his Children's City at Bridge of Weir, there have been many changes, of course, to keep abreast with changing times—especially in the last forty years since the Second World War. The cottage-groups became too large. Sometimes discipline became excessive, even cruel. Brothers and sisters were separated and segregated. The Canadian emigration scheme suffered when examples of gross exploitation and neglect of British children came to light. These were bitter blots on a magnificent record; but they were also milestones in the growth of public acceptance of the need for communal, social responsibility for the helpless in our midst. A century and more after the foundation of Quarrier's Homes, there has been another revolution in ideas about child welfare: children's Homes with a capital H are being shut down all over the place, fostering is now the order of the day, and even the best of the old traditional "institutions" are now regarded with distaste.

The men and women who have carried on Quarrier's work down the years have always been strong on tradition; but they have never been afraid of change. Especially now. In tune with changing demand, Quarrier's is now in the midst of an ambitious and far-sighted **8 Year Plan** to diversify and re-organise its resources. With the need for traditional Children's Homes decreasing rapidly, Quarrier's Homes is being tran.;formed from a Children's City into a unique village community for needy groups of all kinds, both young and old, able and disabled, in a sheltered environment that is nonetheless as normal and free as possible: a village that provides holiday homes for deprived families; a Respite Care Unit to provide short-term care as a relief for the families of profoundly handicapped youngsters; sheltered accommodation for the elderly; leadership courses for teenagers; residential courses for problem youngsters. Some schemes are run in co-operation with the local authority; others are run by charitable organisations, using the splendid facilities provided by Quarrier's.

There is no end to the possibilities for housing all kinds of people with special needs, ranging from expert medical care on tap to the simple need of many to live in a friendly village atmosphere where everyone knows everyone else, and the quiet rhythms of country life have a serenity still that modern urban life so conspicuously lacks.

Environment is all. And Quarrier's is trying to achieve a balanced environment by introducing several small businesses and industries, and commercial housing development as well. It already has all the amenities and infrastructure of a "real" village—church and Post Office, Sports Centre and General Store, shops and offices, council and commuters. It already has its cherished traditions of community and caring. It already has a fascinating past; now it has an equally fascinating future.

The whole concept of a Community of Caring is just as exciting and visionary today as the Children's City that William Quarrier founded, so many years ago and in such different times.

The Village tells the story of these years, these changing times—and the thousands of young lives that were changed. It is much more than a mere tribute to William Quarrier and to the men and women of Quarrier's. It is a story of high hope and heroism, of determination and dedication, of warmth and willingness, of conscience and compassion.

It is a story that lifts the heart.

Magnus Magnusson.

CHAPTER ONE

Beginnings

IT ALL BEGAN more than one hundred and fifty years ago in a small street within sight and sound of the docks of Greenock. It was there, in a close off Crosshore Street — a narrow lane running down to the quayside where lighters loaded their cargo, and steamboats from Glasgow disgorged their passengers — that William Quarrier was born on September 29, 1829.

Greenock, on Scotland's Firth of Clyde, was in 1829 a busy industrial town with an illustrious shipbuilding history. Scott's Shipbuilding and Engineering Company of Greenock, founded in 1711, was one of the many companies which helped to make Greenock the centre of shipbuilding on the Clyde during the eighteenth century. By the early nineteenth century new shipbuilding centres had developed further up the Clyde, notably at Port Glasgow and Dumbarton, but Greenock was still the chief highway to the Atlantic, and every day great ocean-going liners anchored out at the Tail of the Bank. Greenock could also claim fame as the birthplace of the inventor of the steam-engine, James Watt. And now, ten years after his death, another child destined for fame was born.

William Quarrier was the second of three children, and had an older and younger sister. The family had little money and his mother often had to look after the household on her own for long periods while her husband plied his trade as a ship's carpenter, calling at ports all over the world. It was while William's father was working in a ship in

1

James Stewart

Joseph Swan

Customs House Quay, Greenock (Reproduced by Courtesy of GREENOCK CENTRAL LIBRARY)

Quebec that disaster struck. He contracted cholera and died, leaving his family destitute thousands of miles away across the sea. Annie Quarrier had three children to feed and clothe, and no source of income, so she had to try to provide by herself. She opened a small shop in Greenock but it was not successful and, after months of worry and despair at trying to make ends meet, she decided that she would have to move the family to Glasgow and find work there. She scraped together enough for the fares for one of the big steamers which ran daily between Greenock and Glasgow and, one afternoon in 1834, William Quarrier, just five years old, stood with his family on Glasgow's busy Broomielaw quayside where all the big Clyde steamers docked.

Early Victorian Glasgow was in the throes of industrial expansion. The city was superbly placed for trade with the world: down the Clyde lay the route to the Atlantic and commerce with the American continent; to the east, the Forth and Clyde Canal opened the way to the North Sea and Europe. All along the Broomielaw great ships, heavy with cargo, lined the docks five or six deep, waiting to unload their goods and materials from all over the world — timber from South American forests, sugar and rum from the West Indies, fish and chemicals from Europe and Russia. Passenger and cargo steamboats nudged past one another on their way to Liverpool, Belfast and Dublin; and as they went bustling down the river they would meet vessels heading for Glasgow from local resorts all over the Firth, like Millport on the Isle of Cumbrae and Rothesay on the Isle of Bute.

The city's famous Tobacco Lords, once to be seen strolling along the Trongate in their scarlet cloaks, were gone now and in their footsteps walked men whose money lay in Glasgow's new booming industry — cotton: tons and tons of it, pouring into the city for delivery to Scotland's 134 mills, almost all of them within 25 miles of Glasgow. The cotton and textiles industry spawned a host of factories all over the city which employed thousands of men, women and children. Dotted thickly on both sides of the river were spinning and weaving mills, lawn and cambric manufacturers, linen printers and dyers, sewed muslin makers, yarn merchants, chemical and dye works, steam-engine manufacturers. Glasgow also boasted other

Broomielaw in Quarrier's day
(Reproduced by Courtesy of THE MITCHELL LIBRARY)

industries besides cotton; many people worked in the iron, brick and glass works and, in a little village called Govan on the south bank of the river, were the beginnings of marine engineering which was to be the cornerstone of the city's industry from the 1860s onwards.

It was to this expanding, wealthy city that the Quarrier family came to make a new start. But, with very little money, they were forced to live in one of the poorest and most overcrowded areas of the city. Like thousands of others, they experienced the dark side of Glasgow's industrial success and joined the ranks of the city's growing population of poor folk, crowded in dark and dingy tenements amidst factory and mill.

With the expansion of industry and the vast migration of people from rural areas to the city in search of jobs, among them a constant stream of Irish, Glasgow's population had rocketed from 42,832 in 1780 to 110,460 in 1811 and over 200,000 at the beginning of the 1830s. This caused severe overcrowding in certain parts of the city which the authorities simply could not cope with. At that time Glasgow was divided into four completely separate and independent burghs, and there was no one central authority responsible for clearing the overcrowded areas and building better houses. The worst spot was the rectangle of alleys and wynds formed by the Trongate on the north, the Saltmarket and Stockwell Street to the east and west, and the riverside on the south. Time and again since the early years of the century this area had been singled out as a black spot containing the worst elements of appalling housing, insanitary conditions and disease-ridden streets. One particularly strong critic was a Mr. J. C. Symons, a government official who was sent to Glasgow in 1835 to inspect the living conditions of handloom weavers across the river in Paisley. Mr. Symons was so appalled by some of the places he saw in the centre of Glasgow that he could not refrain from including in his report a vivid description of the horrors he encountered:

> The Wynds of Glasgow comprise a fluctuating population of from 15,000 to 20,000 persons. This quarter consists of a labyrinth of lanes, out of which numberless entrances lead into small courts, each with a reeking dunghill in the centre. Revolting as was the outside appearance of these places, I was little prepared for the filth and destitution within. In some of these lodging-houses (visited at night) we found a whole lair of human beings littered along the floor, sometimes fifteen or twenty, some clothed and some naked, men, women and children, huddled promiscuously together. Their bed consisted of a layer of musty straw intermixed with rags. There was generally no furniture in these places.

It was in a close off the teeming High Street, on the edge of this most congested area of the city, that the Quarriers found a room. The High Street, notorious for the length and narrowness of its closes, was one of the four main streets which formed the ancient centre of Glasgow. The Saltmarket, the Trongate, High Street and the Gallowgate all converged at Glasgow Cross. These streets had been the business hub of eighteenth century Glasgow, but by the time the Quarriers arrived the middle-classes had long ago migrated to the west of the city, leaving their once-elegant two and three-storey apartments to house far more people than they were ever meant for.

In their High Street room, Annie Quarrier tried to provide for the family by taking in fine sewing from one of the big warehouses. William helped her by carrying the finished bundles back to the warehouse and collecting more, but there was never enough work for his mother to make ends meet. So, at the age of seven, William was

5

William Quarrier's Birthplace
in Cross Shore Street, Greenock

Note: The archway of stone now forms the War Memorial
just inside main entrance to the Village

sent to work in a factory (probably the one owned by George Stewart, Pin Maker and Wire Drawer) in Graeme Street, near the Gallowgate. For ten or twelve hours a day, six days a week, he sat at a table and fixed the ornamental head tops onto pins and all for the princely sum of one shilling a week. It was not in the least unusual for a child of his age to work those sort of hours. Before the 1833 Factory Act to "Regulate the Labour of Children and Young Persons in Mills and Factories", the normal working day for children from six years upwards in the cotton mills was anything between nine and twelve hours. Young boys and girls were employed as 'scavengers', crawling under the machines to pick up fluff and rubbish, or as 'piecers' whose job was to tie the threads together when they broke. Down in the coalmines, children spent long, damp, dark hours crouched beside the little doors which they had to open when the coal trolleys were sent along the line. In print works, lace factories and matchmaking factories young boys and girls worked alongside men and women, doing a full day's work for small reward. For hundreds of families like the Quarriers, sending the children out to work was the only way of surviving.

But even with William's contribution to the family's budget, the Quarriers were very, very poor. Years later he wrote of the hardships of these early days — in particular, of one day he remembered when he stood in the High Street "barefooted, bareheaded, cold and hungry, having tasted no food for a day and a half". Poverty like that was common on the streets of Glasgow and many were much worse off than the Quarriers. At least William's family had his weekly shilling and whatever his mother earned, but for those with no source of income there was only parish relief. Since the sixteenth century, Scottish parishes gave small amounts of money to those who could prove that they were in need and unable to provide for themselves. The kirk raised the money through voluntary collections, funeral dues and other such means, and this was then distributed among poor families in the parish. In Glasgow money was raised through compulsory assessment of the means of the wealthier members of the town and distributed under the auspices of the Town Hospital.

It must have been very unpleasant to be dependent upon poor relief in nineteenth century Glasgow. Paupers were looked down on by the hard-working, respectable citizens, and the amount of money a person on poor relief was entitled to was usually very little, enough only for a very spartan way of life. And sometimes, not even for that; according to one Donald Ross, an agent of the Glasgow Association in Aid of the Poor, some paupers had to survive on appallingly little, barely enough for food and warmth. Ross compiled a document in 1847 entitled *Pictures of Pauperism:* 'The condition of the poor described by themselves in fifty genuine letters, addressed by paupers to the agent of the Glasgow Association in Aid of the Poor'; in his indignant Preface to the letters, Ross cites the example of an old widow who lived in a tiny apartment. She was:

> without food, without proper clothing, without fuel, and without furniture. She was allowed five shillings per month by the parish, out of which she paid three shillings per month for rent, leaving two shillings a month, or *little more than three farthings a day for food, fuel and clothing!*

According to Ross, such low payments were by no means unusual.

Another feature of the workings of the Poor Law in Scotland which seems very harsh by today's Welfare State standards is that, traditionally, poor relief could only be administered to those who were destitute and *disabled.* In other words, if a man were unemployed but able-bodied he was not officially entitled to parish aid. He might be given a little money in return for some sort of community work — breaking stones on the highway, for instance — or the Poor Inspector might tide him over with something for a day or two, but officially only widows, sick or infirm men, deserted wives, orphans, deserted children and the aged were eligible for relief. This meant great hardship during the periods of mass unemployment, like the 'Hungry Forties', but it stemmed from a widespread attitude that unemployment was somehow the fault of the individual, and that a man without a job simply hadn't looked hard enough for one.

However, those not entitled to poor relief could always fall back on the many charitable organisations and voluntary societies, like the Glasgow Society for Benevolent Visitation of the Destitute Sick and

The High Street, Glasgow (Reproduced by Courtesy of THE MITCHELL LIBRARY)

others in Extreme Poverty, a high-falutin title for a very practical society which issued tickets to poor folk which entitled them to food, clothing and other necessities at certain specified shops all over the city. The New Statistical Account for 1841 listed 33 "Benevolent and Charitable Institutions of Glasgow, exclusive of Widows' Funds, Benefit Societies, Charity Schools and Maintenance of Paupers", and new societies were being formed all the time to try to ease the hardships of poverty and want that so many suffered.

The Quarriers bore their share of hunger and want as they eked out a living, day by day. But William's mother realised that he needed a proper trade to secure his own and the family's future, so when William was about 8 years old she had him apprenticed to a shoemaker in the High Street.

Most of his work consisted of running around after the men in the shop, lighting their pipes, fetching and carrying and preparing the rosined threads for sewing. This did not last for long, however; according to John Urquhart, Quarrier's earliest biographer, the business went bankrupt through the intemperate drinking habits of the owner, so another situation was found for William with a shoemaker in Paisley, on the south side of the river Clyde. This meant he had to walk there and back every day — a distance of some 13 miles. And the shoemaker's apprentice didn't even have a pair of shoes of his own! But William Quarrier was a determined little character, and one cold, dark New Year's Eve he even raced the stage-coach into the city on his way back from work. He doggedly chased it mile after mile, as the coach bumped through the gas-lit streets, and by the time it reached the 'Half-Way House' in Paisley Road West, the passengers were so amazed and delighted by the tenacity of the skinny boy running behind that they started to throw him coins and cheer him on. They dragged William into the warm inn parlour and plied him with food and drink. Then flushed with Hogmanay bonhomie and 'Half-Way House' beer, they ushered him into the coach and paid his fare the rest of the way to Glasgow.

It's a story too irresistibly true to the character of the man to be the mere invention of a devoted biographer. That boy became the young man who, years later, joined Blackfriars Church in Glasgow and, appalled at the poor attendance, determined to do something about it. With great deliberateness he chose an empty pew and week after week invited friends and acquaintances to accompany him to church until the pew was filled. Then he started on the pew behind and repeated the whole process. After a few months, Blackfriars Church was considerably busier than when William Quarrier had joined!

Young William worked hard at his trade and, at only 12, became a journeyman shoemaker. It was a remarkably early age at which to have learned the trade, but such was his application and skill that he had no difficulty in keeping up with the older men in the shop. In the next four years he gained experience and perfected his trade by moving around Glasgow, working for short periods in various boot and shoe shops until he found a situation with a Mrs. Hunter who owned premises in the elegant and fashionable Argyle Street.

By this time William was earning sufficient money to provide his family with better accommodation and he was able to rent a small house in Alston Street (where the Central Station now stands). Gradually he was pulling himself up from the grinding poverty of the early years.

During the years he worked for Mrs. Hunter he was introduced by her to Blackfriars Street Baptist Church. There, at the age of 17, William first declared his Christian faith, a faith awesome in its simplicity and strength. Years later he wrote of his conversion in one of the annual accounts of his work:

> For the first time I heard the great truth of the Gospel, that "God so loved the world that He gave His only begotten Son, that whosoever believeth on Him should not perish, but have everlasting life". Under the influence of the Spirit and teaching of the Word of God, I was led to accept of Christ as all my salvation

And that was it. No fuss, no momentous doubts and struggles to overcome, and yet a faith which was to be the life-long inspiration and motivation of all his work among Scotland's poor and orphaned children.

The second great event of Quarrier's life for which Mrs. Hunter could claim a share of the credit was his marriage to Isabella — Mrs. Hunter's daughter. William courted her for ten years before they finally married in December 1856. By that time William Quarrier was a rising man. He had opened his first boot and shoemaker's shop, at the age of 24, at 243 Argyle Street and this proved so successful that he moved to larger premises further along the street in 1861. William Quarrier seemed set for profitable future in business and, indeed, in the next few years he was to open more bootmaking shops in Glasgow, one in the Gallowgate in 1867 and another in Cowcaddens in 1869, which made him one of the city's first multiple store owners. But by that time he was also involved in work with the poor children of the city, work which made him no money and which would ultimately lead to his giving up the shoemaking business. It all resulted from an incident one winter's night in 1864.

A Glasgow back-court (Reproduced by Courtesy of THE MITCHELL LIBRARY)

CHAPTER TWO

'Like Moses of Old'

IT WAS A COLD, raw night in November 1864, and William Quarrier was walking back home to Kingston Place after a long day's business in the city. As he turned into Jamaica Street and headed towards the Old Bridge he caught sight of a small figure in the shadows at the side of the street. It was a young boy, a match-seller. He was crying bitterly. Quarrier stopped to ask him what was wrong and, between sobs, the lad told him that an older boy had just stolen all his stock and night's earnings while his back was turned,

Quarrier comforted the boy and gave him enough money to replenish his matches, but as he continued on his way, he could not put the incident out of his mind. For some years now, ever since he had started in business for himself and settled into a comfortable way of life, a conviction had been growing inside him, sharpened by his sense of Christian responsibility, that he could not remain all his life just a Glasgow businessman. Every day he saw the city's poor folk, the children on the street corners, day and night, selling newspapers and matches, families singing and begging for pennies, all a constant reminder of his own poor beginnings. He felt a duty to help, as he described years later in the first annual report he published on his work among children:

> Like Moses of old, I had a strong desire to go down to my brethren, the children of the streets, and endeavour to lead them from a life of misery and shame to one of usefulness and honour.

But he felt unfitted for such a great undertaking. Surely someone else would take up the work, someone with abundant means, time and talent? But that night in November, confronted by one of his 'brethren', Quarrier could put off his decision no longer: *he* was the one to do the work, and he would accept the challenge.

So he went home and wrote a letter which appeared in the *Glasgow Herald* on December 2, 1864:

Sir,

On my occasional visits to London I have been much pleased with many of the sights to be seen there, but with none more than with the tidy and clean appearance of the London Shoe-Black Brigade, an institution peculiar to London. There are to be seen many hundreds of youths who have none to care for them, fed, clothed and educated from their own earnings, in brushing boots and shoes, and sent forth into the world to be useful members of society. No doubt many of these youths, if left to themselves, would become wrecks on the great sea of London life, but as it is they are an honour to the nation for industry and perseverance, and these good results may be chiefly attributed to those gentlemen who give a little of their spare time to the management of the Society. Always on my return to Glasgow I have wished that we had such an institution here. I think we have need of it. In almost every street of our city are to be found youths who have none to care for them and possessing all the elements of industry and perseverance. If these were formed into a Glasgow Shoe-Black Brigade the same results as have followed the London institution might be fairly looked for here. Now, sir, if a number of gentlemen would come forward (which I am sure many would be glad to do), I would be happy to be one of them, giving of my time and substance towards this object. I have no doubt, with the aid of your pen and that of your contemporaries; of the success of such an undertaking. Although it might not have an annual revenue of £40,000 like the Great Western Cooking Depot Scheme, yet if it fed, clothed and educated forty destitute youths, preserving them from the vices that surround them, and making them useful members of society, I say that the result would far transcend any pecuniary aid that might be given to it.

Yours truly,

SHOEBLACK.

The response to Quarrier's letter was not overwhelming. Some scoffed that it would never work, that it would be impossible to train street arabs for a worthwhile occupation and, anyway, Glasgow was too rainy for a shoeblack to be able to do business! Nonsense, replied Quarrier; there were already many boys doing just that, but they needed to be organised, educated and looked after. His plan was that the boys would work as part of a uniformed team, charging a ha'penny per shoeshine and giving a percentage of their earnings towards the cost of their stock and uniform, board and lodging if they needed it, and the night classes which Quarrier planned they should all attend.

Provost John Blackie, the head of the well-known Glasgow publishing firm, was one of the first to offer Quarrier his support. Gradually others followed and a committee was formed to plan the work. But Quarrier was not a committee man and had no patience with the deliberations and discussions which ensued. He itched to see his scheme in action and became so irritated at the slow way the matter was proceeding that James Pagan, the editor of the *Glasgow Herald*, remarked to him one day, "Mr. Quarrier, if this work is to be done, you will have to do it yourself".

Quarrier did just that and forged ahead on his own. He began by scouring the stations and street corners where many shoeblacks were to be found and invited some forty of them to his house for tea to discuss his proposition. Most came, and were glad they had done so when they saw the spread of sandwiches and cakes which Mrs. Quarrier had provided. Quarrier wisely waited until they had eaten their fill before outlining his plan. The boys would work during the day and attend reading and writing classes in the evening and Sabbath School each week. At Sabbath School they would practise their reading by learning Scripture texts and reading from the Bible. A hundred years ago such Sabbath Schools were the only way that a great many children could learn to read and write, because they were working the other six days of the week. This was how Quarrier himself had acquired all his early education.

On the financial side, Quarrier explained to the boys that they would receive eight pence out of every shilling they earned. Each boy would be issued with a uniform—a cap and navy-blue flannel jacket trimmed with red, and a red badge on the arm. Every boy would be independent to work at his own pace and wherever he wanted, but would be responsible, too, as part of a team.

After the boys trooped out that evening—helping themselves to one or two little ornaments and valuable-looking objects on the way, as Mrs. Quarrier discovered later—Quarrier's list of names showed that about a third of the group had accepted his offer. The Shoe-Black Brigade of Glasgow was in business.

Headquarters were set up in Jamaica Street, in a room overlooking the Old Bridge. This was close enough to Quarrier's premises in Argyle Street to enable him to oversee things at the Brigade and carry on his own business as well. He engaged a man to teach the evening classes and personally saw to the kitting out of each boy with a uniform, brushes, blacking and all the other tackle of the trade. Then Quarrier's boys took to the streets.

One of the early members of the Brigade was a wild lad called David Grey. He was fifteen when he volunteered for the Brigade, had no money in the world and had pawned most of his clothes. And yet, within a year, David was one of the top earners in the Brigade, sometimes bringing in thirty shillings a week and more, and had lost his reputation for gambling and roughness. He more than vindicated Quarrier's belief that support and organisation would bring out the best in even the most hardened street arab.

As the organisation grew, larger premises were needed. A move was first made to Bath Street and then to a large flat of six apartments at 114 Trongate, in the heart of the city. The membership of the Brigade had risen to a fairly steady 200 and the new premises had ample accommodation for schoolrooms and dormitories. The Brigade was doing well, earning its keep and gaining a reputation among its customers for tidiness, efficiency and good manners. Some years later Quarrier started a Newspaper Brigade, and then a Parcels Brigade, and for all the parcels and boxes entrusted to his boys at stations and offices, there was never once a claim for damage or loss. In fact, the various Brigades were soon so successful that certain business interests in the city became rather alarmed. Some newspaper offices were not happy when Quarrier demanded reduced rates for his newspaper boys because, he said, he was a wholesaler, taking some 4,000 copies a day. And the licensed City Porters were none too thrilled at competition from the Parcels Brigade.

But, despite these frictions, Quarrier's Brigades continued to operate in the streets of Glasgow until the turn of the century, offering help, support and training to hundreds of young boys.

A Typical Glasgow Close: No. 118 High Street
(Reproduced by Courtesy of THE MITCHELL LIBRARY)

By 1870 William Quarrier had a string of shoe and boot shops in Glasgow and, between running his business and organising his Brigades, he was an extremely busy man. He had recently moved house to Kingston Place, on the south side of the city, and had a large household to support—his wife and four children, as well as the children of his younger sister whose husband had died; when his sister died soon after her husband, Quarrier took care of the three children and brought them up as his own.

And yet Quarrier's work with the street boys of Glasgow had only convinced him that much more needed to be done. The city around him was a great metropolis of over 450,000 souls, the second city of the Empire. Shipbuilding was growing and replacing the cotton trade as the city's main industry. The boundaries of the city were creeping further and further westwards and southwards and the slums of Quarrier's childhood were at last coming under the scrutiny of the public authorities with the establishment of the City Improvement Trust. The physical face of Glasgow had changed considerably since he was a young boy working in the Graeme Street pin factory; now, too, there was much more public concern about the plight of working children, and of those orphaned and homeless. Conditions in the cotton mills and in the coal mines had been greatly improved by legislation regulating the number of working hours and the ages at which children could be employed. Since 1840 it had been illegal to employ anyone under twenty-one to go down the chimneys and the days of sending young boys of seven or eight down narrow smoky flues were past. Homeless children under fifteen could now be taken off the streets by the courts and sent to Industrial Schools all over Scotland where they would be fed and clothed and trained for a trade.

But though much had been achieved, the children of the streets remained. Quarrier saw them daily as he walked to work, when he visited his Brigade boys at their various posts around the city, and when he returned home at night. The same children that Dickens has etched on our imaginations—Oliver Twist on the road to London, David Copperfield buying his ha'penny lunch of a stale pie after working for hours in the blacking factory, Jo the crossing sweeper in *Bleak House*, alone from morning to night, with no home and no family—were a fact of life on the streets of Glasgow. Some had lost one or both parents through the common diseases of tuberculosis, bronchitis and cholera; others were sent out to beg and steal for the family; others had simply left home and lived on the streets. The writer of the 1841 Statistical Account entry on Glasgow had noted that:

> . . . the number of orphans, and, what is worse, the number of children of depraved parents, thrown on the public without anyone to care for them, almost exceeds belief. *(p217)*

By the last quarter of the century the situation was no better. Town authorities placed some children in the Poorhouse and boarded out many on farms or crofts in rural districts, but still the city's streets were full of homeless children and the reports of the Glasgow Society for the Prevention of Cruelty to Children, formed in 1884, recount case after case of children found wandering the streets, sleeping on stairheads and boxes and huddled against baker's ovens. The following two cases are taken from a long list in the Society's 1886 Annual Report:

> *Case 114* M.G., a girl of twelve years of age, was found begging by the Superintendent and taken to the Shelter. On enquiries being made into her case it was found that both her parents were dead, and she was living by begging, without any proper home or guardian.

> *Case 203* D. McLean, twelve years of age. This boy was found selling papers and begging late at night by the officers of the Society. He stated that he had been supporting himself by begging, selling papers and carrying parcels at railway stations for a considerable time. His mother was dead and his father had deserted him. He had to sleep on stairs when he could not earn sufficient money to pay for his lodgings.

Quarrier wanted to help these children, not just by organising them into industrial brigades, but by giving them a home and the chance of a life away from the dangers and hardships of the streets. He had long had at the back of his mind a plan for a children's Home in Glasgow. He knew of the work of George Müller, a Prussian pastor who had come to England in 1829 and opened an orphanage in Bristol six years later; he knew of Thomas Barnardo, who was labouring among the children of London's teeming streets. And he had met the formidable Annie Macpherson, a young woman from Glasgow who

Tontine Building, Trongate 1868 (Reproduced by Courtesy of THE MITCHELL LIBRARY)

went to London in 1866 to work among the poor people of the East End. In an empty warehouse in the city's Commercial Street she had set up a House of Industry where hundreds of child matchbox-makers could work at their trade and receive food and education at the same time. Quarrier had met her when she visited Glasgow at the end of the 1860s, and was impressed with her account of the work in London; he was especially interested to hear of her Canadian emigration scheme for orphaned and destitute children which she had started in 1869. She believed that such children would have a better chance in life if they were taken away from their miserable and impoverished surroundings and shipped out to work as farm-hands and domestics in homesteads in Canada. Annie urged Quarrier to put his plans for a children's Home into immediate action, and brushed aside his worries that he already had too much on his plate, with his business, his family and his Brigades: God would support the work, she declared, and others would rally round.

Quarrier made up his mind to go ahead and on August 31, 1871, a second historic letter appeared in the *Glasgow Herald*. On September 1st, the same letter, with minor variations, was published in the *North British Daily Mail:*

Sir,

For many years past I have been deeply impressed with the necessity that exists here for a Home for destitute boys, and I am persuaded that there is no one who moves about and notices the habits and surroundings of the boys of our streets but will be convinced that such a home is needed. Many of your readers may not be aware of the vast number of houseless and homeless boys who receive shelter in our Night Asylum, and as this is one reason why we should have a Home, I beg to put before them the number who have received shelter during the past year which is, according to the report, 3,397. Giving three nights to each boy (which is the allotted time in the institution), this would give the number of 1,137 boys who either roam our streets or country without a home to cheer their desolate lives, or a house to cover their defenceless heads. Some have an easy way of getting out of their Christian responsibilities, and they say of these helpless ones, 'Send them to the Poorhouse'; others, to quiet their consciences, give a copper when they see the haggard face and tattered garments of the little urchin, and so the stream of neglected children goes on, deepening and deepening until God only knows what length it may reach. Fellow Christians and fellow citizens, should such things continue? I would say no, and thus I plead for a Home to which any boy may be sent, his case enquired into, and a helping hand extended to him, until he is fit to labour for himself. It is only by such means that crime can be lessened in our juvenile population; for criminals are of the worst class who are so from their youth, and cost the country a thousand times more for the cure than for the prevention of crime. In fact, I believe it can't be cured, but I am sure that it might be prevented—not to speak of the disgrace to us that so many destitute children should be allowed to roam as they like amongst us, without let or hindrance. The amount of help rendered to the destitute boys of our streets by the Shoe-Black Society has been of great use to them, and many hundreds have received help which has been a blessing to themselves and to the community, but one great want has been a Home to which orphan and destitute boys might be sent at once by any citizen who found them so, and to which an emigration scheme might be attached, so as to draft off to another land, all who were fitted for it. Miss Macpherson, of London, has promised her practical co-operation and, with such help, there is no fear of success. Shall the practical help and sympathy of my fellow-citizens be wanting? I have no faith in large institutions where hundreds are ruled with a stringent uniformity which eats out the individuality of its members, but I have great faith in a Home where not more than one hundred are placed together, and where individual tastes would be cared for and watched over by a motherly and fatherly love. The Home I think we should begin with might cost from £1,000 to £2,000 to build and fit out, and if any of my fellow-citizens would feel inclined to put out this sum or any amount towards it, I feel certain that it would be laying up treasure in Heaven, where neither moth nor rust doth corrupt, and the blessing of those who are ready to perish would be sure to fall on their heads. The establishment of such a Home at the present time would be a fitting stone of remembrance of the Earl of Shaftesbury's visit to our city, and I have no doubt would meet with his hearty support and co-operation. Any communications or subscriptions towards the above object shall be duly acknowledged by

Yours truly,

W. Quarrier

It's a marvellous letter, at once passionate, practical and radical: by declaring, in an age of barrack-like workhouses, that he had no faith in large institutions but believed, instead, in preserving the individual, William Quarrier identified himself unmistakably as a man ahead of his time.

Just twelve days later Quarrier received a letter promising the necessary money to buy or rent premises for the new Home. It came from a London businessman called Thomas Corbett. Corbett was already familiar with Quarrier's work with the Brigades, and Quarrier had written to him personally about the need for an orphanage in Glasgow.

With the problem of money taken care of, Quarrier lost no time in looking for a suitable site for his home and found it in Renfrew Lane, a little street running parallel to Sauchiehall Street. The place was small—just an old workshop—but Quarrier partitioned it off into a kitchen and sleeping area and tried to brighten up the bare brick walls with illuminated texts from the Bible. The matron of the new home was a Mrs. Dunn. Like many other women who helped with sewing, mending, cooking and teaching, she had volunteered to work in the Home. Quarrier had met her some months before in Porteous's Bookshop in Royal Exchange Square, where she worked and which he used to visit from time to time. One day he told her of his plans for a Home, and asked if she would help out if his scheme materialized. She had promised her support, and for eight years she acted as Matron to hundreds of girls and boys.

Now the Renfrew Lane Home was ready to open and on November

22

18, 1871, the first boy stepped tentatively over the threshold. His name was Andrew, he had no jacket or shoes, and his first words as he padded across to the brightly-burning fire in the corner were to enquire where everyone else was. He was followed the day after by Willie, a young boy, filthy and ragged, who had spent the last few nights in a cold tenement stairway. They were joined soon after by Jimmy, an orphan who had been deserted by his aunt and uncle and who scraped a living on the streets by selling matches and standing on his head for a ha'penny.

And so the list of names grew and the trickle of orphans and waifs became a stream. They ranged in age from four to fourteen; some were found by Quarrier and his helpers among the barrels and boxes at the harbour, in haylofts and stairways; some were brought, in varying degrees of wretchedness, filth and hunger, by missionary women and policemen; others turned up on the doorstep by themselves. Preference was given to orphans, then the children of widows, and lastly the children of dissolute parents willing to hand them over into Quarrier's care. Every case was carefully enquired into—which sometimes ended up with a boy or girl being sent back to perfectly worthy parents from whom they'd run away out of mischief.

A year after its opening the Renfrew Lane Home was so full that new premises had to be found. The boys were sent to Cessnock House, an old mansion house in spacious grounds in Govan Road, on the south side of the city, and the girls to new premises at 93 Renfield Street. Later this home moved to another house, also in Govan Road. Corbett's original donation contributed towards the new houses and the rest was provided by money sent in by the public. One of Quarrier's worries about starting a Home of this kind had been money; he certainly could not afford to finance the work single-handed and each day children would have to be fed and clothed. But the money did come. Every day, gifts of a few pence, a shilling, or several pounds poured in from all over the country: 'B.E., Glasgow, a sincere sympathiser, £10'; 'a Working Man, in stamps, 1s'; 'a Friend, Bridge of Allan, 5s' — in that first year alone, £1,399 15 3. As well as money, every day saw clothing, crockery, materials, food and furniture arriving from as far afield as London and Aberdeen. There is even a note in the 1872 Annual Report of 'a fine milk cow for Cessnock House', sent by Miss T. of Hillhead.

In the first year, 93 children entered the home at Renfrew Lane. 35 were sent to Canada as part of Annie Macpherson's emigration scheme (cf Chapter 5), one girl was adopted, two boys were drafted into the Shoe-Black Brigade, two returned to friends, one poor boy was sent to the Poorhouse because he was mentally unstable, and two boys ran away. At the end of the first year the Renfrew Lane Home was abandoned and every child was transferred either to Cessnock House or Renfield Street, which together had accommodation for about 100. The day-to-day routine at both places consisted of a mixture of formal lessons and chores or domestic tasks. With some 50 or 60 children in each home, it was difficult to maintain much of the atmosphere of a family household which was Quarrier's ideal, but he saw to it that the children played together, helped around the house and worshipped together, morning and evening.

Most of the children in Cessnock House and Renfield Street did not stay for long, but were almost immediately shipped off to Canada. But Quarrier also wanted to provide the means for rescuing children from the streets and training them for future lives and employment at home in Scotland. To do this, he had a plan for a new and special Home.

Jamaica Bridge (Reproduced by Courtesy of THE MITCHELL LIBRARY)

CHAPTER THREE

Depriving the Poorhouse

. . . My early dreams and life's desire have been partly accomplished in the establishment of the Orphan Homes, but as there are a great many orphan children whom we have not been able to take up, and whom it is desirable to keep at home and train to useful occupations, I would like to see an Orphanage established near Glasgow on the cottage principle, to which children from any part of the country could be sent. By the cottage principle, I mean a number of cottages built near each other, say ten, each capable of accommodating 20 to 30 children, with a father and mother at the head of each household; playground and other appliances attached to each cottage, with a schoolhouse in the centre; also a central workshop; the father of each family to be able to teach a different trade, such as tailor, shoemaker, joiner, printer, baker, farmer, smith, etc; the mother to do the cooking for each household, with assistance if needed. Boys from the tailor's household, wishing to learn shoemaking, could be sent to the shoemaker's workshop; or boys from the farmer's household, wishing to learn joiner work, could be sent to the joiner's workshop; and so on, interchanging according to the trade best suited to the boy. The children would meet all together at school and church, and on special occasions in the common playground, but at other times in their own playground. It is desirable to keep up the family and home feeling amongst the children, and we believe this cannot be done in large institutions where hundreds of children are ruled by the stringent uniformity necessary where large numbers are gathered together for years.

This was William Quarrier's plan for a new Home, described in the first *Narrative of Facts* — an annual account of his work — in 1872. He was proposing nothing less than the construction of an entire village for children, complete with houses, shops and a school. It was a bold ambitious scheme which must have caused even William

25

Quarrier moments of doubt when he contemplated all the money and labour involved; he calculated that the purchase of the land and construction of the buildings would cost £20,000, a truly enormous sum in those days. Many skilled men and women would be needed and a vast amount of planning and work would be necessary in the selection of a suitable site.

And yet, for all its scale and magnitude, this latest plan was the natural progression and development of Quarrier's work. He had started with Industrial Brigades to organise and support the many young boys who scraped a meagre living on the streets. Then had come the Homes in Renfrew Lane and later Govan Road which gave shelter to hundreds of homeless and orphaned children and tried to help them to a better life — by sending them to Canada, or placing them in situations at home, recruiting them for the Brigades or just providing a roof over their heads until something could be found. Now Quarrier wanted to give the children a more permanent home where they could live and grow, somewhere that looked and felt more like home than a Home. Of course by modern standards, 20 or 30 children in one cottage is far too many — today some of the cottages at Quarrier's Homes have as few as 7 children; but by comparison with the orphanages and poorhouses of his day, where hundreds ate together in huge halls and slept in large impersonal dormitories, the numbers Quarrier was proposing were innovatively small.

The idea of housing orphaned and needy children in cottages was not entirely new. There were no examples of it in Scotland, but Quarrier probably knew of the work of a Miss Meredith in England, who founded the Princess Mary's Village in Addlestone, Surrey, in 1871; there, girls lived in groups of ten in cottages run by a housemother and assisted by an older girl. The original idea for cottage homes had come from the continent; one example was the 'Rauhes Haus' of the German theologian Johann Wichern, opened near Hamburg in 1833. This was a group of cottages where young boys who had been in trouble or had crimnal tendencies lived together in small groups under supervision.

Quarrier was not alone in his conviction that large institutions were not the place to bring up children and that they needed to be in smaller groups in a homelier, more intimate atmosphere. Dr. Barnardo was to come to the same conclusion just a few years later when he opened his first cottage home for girls at Barkingside, Essex, in 1876; his previous experience of running a large orphanage had shown him that 60 girls living under the same roof had no chance of improving and developing. He eventually decided that a more family-like set-up with smaller numbers was needed, and in his memoirs he described his new vision:

> There should be no longer a great house in which sixty of these motherless girls would be herded together, clad in some dull uniform generally divested of all prettiness; but little cottages should arise, each of them presided over by its own "mother" and in which all the members of the family could be clad as working people's children were under ordinary circumstances. The girls should be of all ages, from the baby of a few months or weeks to the growing girls, some of whom would be nearly out of their teens. There family life and family love might be reproduced, and gentle, modest ways would be made possible in the retirement of the cottage with its four or five rooms, and under the influence of godly women whom I was sure would come to my aid in due time.

Quarrier's original plan was for cottages to accommodate between 20 and 30 children of different ages. Each cottage would be headed by men and women with a committed Christian faith (this was the main stipulation) — a married couple for the boys' cottages and a single woman for the girls'. The children would all help around the house, cleaning, washing, making beds, the older ones helping with the cooking and looking after the young ones. Each cottage would function independently of the others, as a family household, but the children would mix at school and church. In these family groups with firm discipline, congenial surroundings and a strong dose of Christian teaching, Quarrier believed that even the most wretched and the roughest of children could be trained and educated and given a chance for a better future.

£20,000 was a huge sum of money to raise, and the initial response was very slow. By the following year only £88 had been sent in. But Quarrier was confident that the rest would come, just as everything necessary arrived daily for the feeding, clothing and educating of the 180 children admitted so far to the Glasgow Homes. In the meantime Quarrier had other schemes afoot. The first Saturday of 1873 had seen

" Inasmuch as ye have done it unto one of the least of these, ye have done it unto me."

A NARRATIVE OF FACTS

RELATIVE TO WORK DONE FOR CHRIST

IN CONNECTION WITH THE

ORPHAN AND DESTITUTE CHILDREN'S

EMIGRATION HOMES, GLASGOW,

FOR THE YEAR ENDING 31st OCTOBER, 1873.

BY

WILLIAM QUARRIER.

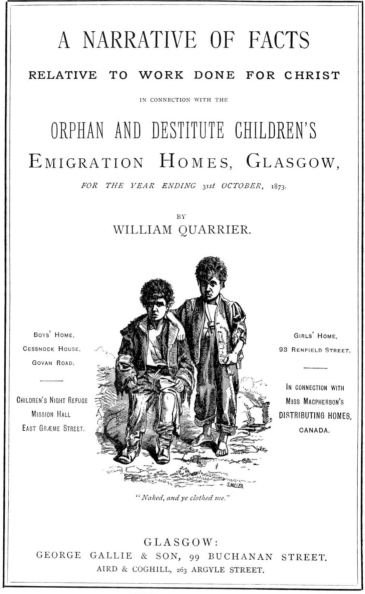

BOYS' HOME,
CESSNOCK HOUSE,
GOVAN ROAD.

———

CHILDREN'S NIGHT REFUGE
MISSION HALL
EAST GRÆME STREET.

GIRLS' HOME,
93 RENFIELD STREET.

———

IN CONNECTION WITH
MISS MACPHERSON'S
DISTRIBUTING HOMES,
CANADA.

" Naked, and ye clothed me."

GLASGOW:

GEORGE GALLIE & SON, 99 BUCHANAN STREET.

AIRD & COGHILL, 263 ARGYLE STREET.

PRICE THREEPENCE.

The cover page of Quarrier's second annual report

the opening of his Night Refuge for children and working lads. This was the first of its kind in Glasgow. There was already a City Night Asylum which took in some children, but it was mainly for men and women. Quarrier's Night Refuge was housed in the upper storey of an old church at the top of Dovehill, bordering Graeme Street, where he had worked as a boy. The floor was partitioned off into a large public area, a kitchen and a dormitory with 20 beds. In the first ten months of its existence the Refuge gave shelter to 2,137 refugees — or rather, provided 2,137 'bed nights'; some children came for more than one night, and these Quarrier tried to help by sending them to his Brigades or to the Govan Road Homes. In the hall, which could accommodate 400 people, Quarrier held twice-weekly evangelistic meetings which were open to the public. The hall was also used as a Reading Room for working men, and once a week there were "sewing nights" for widows who needed to earn a little extra money. The sight of the women must have stirred memories for Quarrier of the many nights, all those years ago in a High Street close, which his mother had spent painstakingly sewing tiny buttons and frills onto muslin and silk.

By 1874 Quarrier had several branches of work going on in the city: his Industrial Brigades were thriving, the Homes in Govan Road continued to send children to Canada, and the Dovehill Mission opened its doors every day to the hungry, the homeless, the poor and the widowed. By this time, too, there was enough money in the cottage homes kitty for Quarrier to start looking for a suitable site. He had £4,688 in hand with which to buy some land near Glasgow, in pleasant countryside, somewhere big enough for future expansion and with plenty of open space for the children. Part of Lord Blantyre's estate at Cardonald, on the southern boundary of the city (the site now occupied by Craigton cemetery), seemed to fit the bill. Quarrier began negotiations to buy the land in December 1874, but the bill of sale was never signed. The *Narrative of Facts* for that year gives no explanation for the breakdown of the deal, but Alexander Gammie in his book *A Romance of Faith* writes that it was on account of a wall which Lord Blantyre insisted should be built round the land he was selling. Quarrier was agreeable to this but only on condition that the wall was not entirely on **his** side, and that Lord Blantyre built part of it on his. This, Lord Blantyre flatly refused to do, so Quarrier decided to look elsewhere.

The breakdown in negotiations occurred in May, 1875, and it was not until nearly a year later that another site was chosen. At the beginning of April, 1876, an advertisement appeared in the newspapers announcing the sale of Nittingshill farm near the little Renfrewshire village of Bridge of Weir. The sale was to be held on April 26; so on a cold, rainy day earlier that month Quarrier travelled out to Bridge of Weir to have a look at the land. The village was about 16 miles from the centre of Glasgow, and the farm of Nittingshill lay 2 miles beyond that. Even in the pouring rain it was a beautiful spot: 40 acres of rich green fields and woodland, with the rolling Kilbarchan hills to the south and the rivers Cattie and Gryffe forming a natural boundary to the estate. Here the children would be deep in the Renfrewshire countryside, and yet there was easy connection with Glasgow by rail.

It was everything Quarrier had been looking for; as he stood surveying the land, in his mind's eye he could see his little village taking shape. There would be an administrative block in the centre, with a communal hall, schoolrooms and workshops. He would range the 10 cottages in a rough circle round the central building, each with its own garden and connected by wide avenues. And then there would be space for cultivating crops to feed the big family and, of course, a playing area. Yes, it was the perfect spot.

The day of the sale found Quarrier excited and hopeful that there would be no competition from other buyers. However, there was another interested buyer who bid against him consistently and Quarrier soon found that he was not to get his land without a bit of a tussle. Slowly the price increased by £5 and £10 , see-sawing from one man to the other, until Quarrier eventually won and bought the 40 acres for £3,560 — £560 more than the reserve price. He immediately vested the land with a group of trustees, among them Thomas Corbett, the man who had donated the original £2,000 for Renfrew Lane.

This same group of men also acted as trustees for another piece of

The City Home, James Morrison Street

land Quarrier had acquired earlier in the year when he had opened his City Home in James Morrison Street, a purpose-built five-storey apartment block which housed the entire Dovehill organisation. The premises at Dovehill had been bought by the School Board, but thanks to the great generosity of two Glasgow ladies who met the entire cost of £10,000, new ground at James Morrison Street was bought and built upon. These remarkably generous women are not named in the *Narrative of Facts* but Alexander Gammie in *A Romance of Faith* identifies them as a Mrs. Robert Smith and her daughter, Mrs. Alexander Allan.

All in all, 1867 was a good year for William Quarrier. He had his new City Home, with accommodation for 100 working lads and temporary shelter for 40 destitute women, a shelter for homeless children and a mission hall. Most importantly, he had at last purchased the ground for Scotland's first cottage homes for children.

The next thing was to start building. Quarrier and his architect, Robert Bryden, envisaged the Central Building in a functional Gothic style with turreted roof, pointed gables and plain uncarved walls. The building would be three-storied with schoolrooms, workrooms and storerooms on the ground floor. The first floor would have a large hall for services and rooms for the teachers. Until there were enough cottages Quarrier also intended using the top floor for sleeping quarters for the children. The plan was for the Homes to be formally opened once the Central Building and two cottages, one on either side, had been completed. Each cottage would be built in a style harmonising with the Central Building, but Quarrier also specified that the cottages were all to be slightly different from one another so as to be more like individual houses with their own characters. He also wanted them to reflect the national character of the Homes. They were to be for children from every part of Scotland, so he suggested in the 1876 *Narrative of Facts* that different towns and cities across the country should donate the money to build a cottage which would be named after them. Individuals might want to build a cottage in memory of a relative, and organisations, such as the Sabbath Schools of Scotland, could use their collection money specially for a cottage at Bridge of Weir.

Although Quarrier made the financial needs of his organisation known to the readers of his *Narrative of Facts* he would not advertise publicly for funds, unlike, for example, Dr. Barnardo in London, who was a great showman and publiciser of his work. Quarrier would approve no fund-raising bazaars or musical entertainments or any other advertising efforts, and he would not employ collectors. He believed that the work in which he was engaged was God's work and that a simple statement of needs in the *Narrative of Facts* and constant prayer would secure whatever was necessary. To this day Quarrier's Homes never advertise for donations or hold fund-raising campaigns.

But William Quarrier was not a man to pray and leave it at that. He was a successful businessman, a man of tremendous energy, enthusiasm and determination who worked tirelessly towards his goals. There is a story told about him by Alexander Gammie in *A Romance of Faith* which perfectly illustrates Quarrier's balance between faith and self-help:

> One Monday morning Mr. Quarrier was driving the weekend preacher to Bridge of Weir station. As they entered the village, the train was seen approaching, and it seemed doubtful if they would be in time. The preacher, in his anxiety lest he should lose the train, excitedly exclaimed: 'Don't you think we should pray about it, Mr. Quarrier?' 'No, not yet' replied Mr. Quarrier, as he cracked the reins, 'wait till we see what the horse can do'. *(p144)*

(For me, that's the real man. I can almost hear the grim amusement in his tone as he restrains his friend's anxious fervour).

Quarrier's architect, Robert Bryden, worked hard at the plans for the new cottage homes and building began in February 1877 with the laying of the foundation-stone of the first cottage. It was to be called 'Broadfield' and the £1,300 for its construction had been promised in a letter which Quarrier had received just six months after the purchase of Nittingshill. The money was gifted by a couple from Port Glasgow in memory of their son; in June of the following year another £1,300 was donated by a lady from Glasgow, in memory of her mother, for a second cottage, to be called 'Glasgow Home'.

Building went on throughout 1877 and by early 1878 work on the Central Building was well under way. The total cost was to be £4,800; but the building fund was short by some £1,300 and when the balance

ORPHAN COTTAGE HOMES OF SCOTLAND.

TO HOUSE 300 ORPHAN AND DESTITUTE CHILDREN, TO COST £20,000.

CHILDREN'S COTTAGE.

The above is a sketch of one of the proposed Cottages prepared by a friend. The house is about 39 feet square. The ground floor consists of parlour, 15 by 12 feet, for father, mother, and visitors; children's nursery or play-room, 18 by 14 feet; dining-room, 18 by 14 feet; kitchen, 14 by 12 feet; scullery, pantry, bath-room, &c. Top flat consists of bed-room for father and mother, 15 by 12 feet; No. 1 dormitory, 18 by 14 feet; No. 2 dormitory, 18 by 14 feet; No. 3 dormitory, 14 by 12 feet; spare bed-room, 7½ by 6 feet; wall wardrobes for children's clothing, &c. Each cottage is to accommodate not more than thirty children, and the expected cost is about £1000.

Reproduced from the 1875 Narrative of Facts

was still outstanding by springtime, Robert Bryden became rather anxious. He suggested to Quarrier that work should be suspended until the rest of the money materialised, but the answer was no: Quarrier believed the money would come in time.

This was a trying time for Quarrier; he was not made any easier in his mind by the prospect of having to leave the scene at this critical stage, for he was due to accompany that year's party of children to Canada — the seventh group of children to make the journey since the Renfrew Lane Home opened. The departure date was May 2, and by late April the outstanding £1,300 had still not appeared. Quarrier had never been away from his work for more than a week; now he was going to be on the other side of the Atlantic for two or three months. It was not that people like Robert Hunter, the Superintendent of Cessnock Home, or the Matron of Renfield Home or the many volunteers who helped in the work were not competent; but it was hard for Quarrier to leave others in charge of all the projects which he had conceived, planned, organised and directed from the beginning. But his wife was particularly anxious for him to have a break from the constant strain of running everything, and, besides, some changes were being made in the Canadian end of the emigration scheme which made it necessary for him to go out and oversee things.

Two days before the *S.S. Phoenician* was due to steam out from Mavisbank Quay (on the south bank of the river), Quarrier received a visit from a friend called Alexander Thomson, a retired farmer and bachelor, who had taken a keen interest in the Homes work from the outset. "I had been intending to give £1,300 for the erection of a cottage" he said, " but I'd like to donate it towards the Central Building instead". So the Central Building account was finally balanced and Quarrier could look forward to the official opening of his new Orphan Homes soon after he returned from Canada in July.

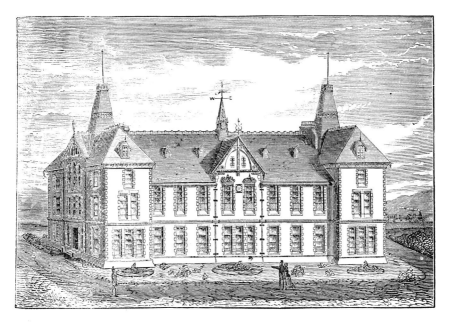

Central Building

September 17, 1878, was the date announced in the newspapers for the official opening of "Mr. Quarrier's Orphan Homes of Scotland at Bridge of Weir". The wet, stormy weather which caused some damage to the roof of the newly-completed Central Building did not deter the hundreds of people who flocked there on the great day. They crammed the special train from Glasgow and arrived in droves from Greenock, Port Glasgow and all over the country. Well before the official proceedings began at 2 o'clock the hall was jammed tight with people; many stood in the aisles and others, crowded together at the back of the hall, had to crane their necks for a view of the platform party.

Quarrier made a sparkling address to the hundreds gathered there that day, among them Dr. Barnardo and Provost Lyle of Greenock. He stood before them, correct and sombre in his dark frock coat, his shrewd, rather stern gaze warm with enthusiasm, and declared, "I am here to testify that God has not failed me at any time". He talked of hope and faith in the future and of the gifts of people from all over the country which had made the day possible, from "the widow's mite to the merchant prince's thousand". He told his listeners that in the last seven years, 700 children had been rescued from the streets of Glasgow and £34,000 had been donated to feed, clothe, educate and look after them. And, in an aside especially designed to encourage businessmen, he revealed that only five per cent of that money had been spent on helpers and workers.

Everyone who heard him must have been stirred by his energy and vision. His plan was for ten cottages to be built in the next few years, but his strong hope was that during his lifetime or after, many more would be added. Looking around the hall he declared, "My earnest desire is to deprive the poorhouse of as many children as possible"; and with thunderous applause ringing in his ears, William Quarrier looked boldly to the future.

Mr. and Mrs. Quarrier

Classes in the old schoolroom of the Central Building (Reproduced from Urquhart's "The Life-Story of William Quarrier")

CHAPTER FOUR

A Children's City

JUST FOUR YEARS after the grand opening of the Orphan Homes of Scotland, William Quarrier had achieved his goal of ten cottages. The original nucleus of buildings—the Central Building, Broadfield Home, Glasgow Home and an unfinished third cottage, Dalry Home— had been joined by seven more cottages—the Dunbartonshire, Ebenezer, Washington, Aberdeen, Greenock, Anderston and Paisley Homes, each the gift of an individual and together housing about 300 children, from toddlers to 12-year-olds.

And Quarrier had surpassed his original dream, by giving the village an invalid's home and a complex of buildings housing workshops and washing facilities. He also had promises of more gifts to build more cottages.

In fact the Orphan Homes of Scotland were so successful and growing at such a rate, that Quarrier even had to give up his shoemaking business in Glasgow and devote himself entirely to the work. He was the motivating force, the inspiration and the sole manager of a vast organisation which now stretched from the smoky centre of Glasgow to the green hills of Renfrewshire and across the Atlantic to Canada. The increasing workload had forced him to give up one of his three shops as early as 1875, and four years later he relinquished another part of his business. Finally, in 1882, he decided that the last of his shops would have to go; eighteen hours a day spent managing the Orphan Homes simply left no time to run a business.

But where was his own income to come from? His friends pointed out that he had always been sublimely confident that all the necessary money for the Homes would come from God when needed—so why not rely on the same source to provide for the needs of himself and his family and trust that money would be sent in specifically for that purpose? Quarrier announced his decision in the *Narrative of Facts* of 1882:

> I believe God will supply, so have decided to depend on Him in the time to come for all that I require for myself and family. This explanation is necessary, as some are under the impression that I have money invested and that I live partly off the Homes. Such is not the case. I have no invested capital, nor have I ever, at any time, lived off the Homes. The opposite is the fact, as a considerable portion of my own means has been given and spent in the interests of the work. For the future I have resolved to continue in the same course, i.e., not to touch anything belonging to the Homes but to depend entirely on the Lord to send what I require for myself and family. I do not say everyone should do as I have done, but if they are led by the Lord in the same way as I have been there is no other course left open to them.

Four years later money was sent in to build a house on the premises at Bridge of Weir for Quarrier and his family to live in. They called it 'Homelea' and it is still there today, just inside the main drive.

A sketch from the 1896 Narrative of Facts

The Orphan Homes of Scotland continued to grow. In 1884 three new cottages—Cessnock, Mizpah and Leven—were completed to house the children from the Govan Road Homes which were now proving too small and were discontinued. At the dedication service for these latest cottages Quarrier declared:

> We have only touched the borders of the orphans of the land. They are there by the thousand. I intend, God willing, to double the number of cottages — that is to say, instead of 17 houses, to have 34. In other words, instead of spending as we have been doing £40,000 in these buildings, we intend to spend £80,000.

He was as good as his word and as cottage followed cottage, and acre after acre of land was drained, levelled and built upon, by the early years of the 1890's the target of 34 cottages was in sight. What had once been 40 green acres of Nittingshill farm was now a thriving community of 46 buildings and over 800 children—a "children's city" as the *North British Daily Mail* called it in an article of 1890. Anyone could come and visit, every day of the week except Sunday. A train from St. Enoch's in Glasgow would whisk the visitor to Bridge of Weir. From there it was a short carriage ride to the Orphan Homes where the Superintendent, Mr. McFadzean, would give a guided tour.

At the main entrance to the Homes were two great gates (no longer there) which opened inwards onto a broad avenue lined with young trees and shrubs and stretching away to the Central Building in the distance. This was Faith Avenue. To the right and left, along its length, stood cottage after cottage, each with its own front lawn and flower patch—Oswald Invalid Home for Girls, Paisley Home, Aberdeen Home, Washington Home. Over to the right down by the Cattie Burn was the laundry and next door the workshops, always a hive of activity, where joiners, printers, shoemakers and bakers, most of them cottage fathers, worked all day.

Further on, a gently sloping road led up Faith Avenue to Mount Zion—a hugh church in Victorian style, with a 120-foot tower. The church was built in 1888 with £5,000 from an anonymous donor. With a seating capacity of 1,000 it could cope with the growing family of children and provided grander surroundings for the services that had previously been held in the Central Building. All around Mount Zion

39

OPENING OF NEW CHURCH AT BRIDGE-OF-WEIR HOMES.
(Reprinted from " North B. itish Daily Mail," 7th March, 1888.)

A large and handsome church, which has been planted amid the Orphan Homes of Scotland at Bridge-of-Weir, was opened yesterday. The event was rightly regarded by Mr. Quarrier, the founder of that most interesting of all colonies, as one of great importance in the history of the beneficent work to which he has devoted all his means, his time, his great organising power, and his marvellous faith. The visible results of that work must appear almost incredible to those who only hear about and don't see them. Since it began 17 years ago, 5,000 children have passed through these Homes and the Homes in Glasgow, and of these 2,500 have been sent to Canada with a full stock of health, a capital training, and plenty of good clothes. On the property, beautifully situated among the Renfrewshire hills, some two miles from Bridge-of-Weir, where the country Homes are, there was only a farmhouse twelve years ago. Now, however, the old farmhouse has disappeared, and there are on the ground

No fewer than 28 Buildings

Reproduced from the 1888 Narrative of Facts

were more cottages facing on to Hope Avenue and behind that, Love Avenue—Montrose Home, Allan Dick Home, Edinburgh Home and many others.

Every cottage and each gift of money had a story behind it. The Sabbath School Home was built with the thousands and thousands of pennies collected by Sabbath Schools all over Scotland. Jehovah-Jireh Home was the result of an anonymous donation of £2,000 in banknotes which was left one morning on Quarrier's desk. Another morning he found among his mail a large bulky envelope which contained dozens and dozens of banknotes totalling £1,700, and a note which said simply, "From Sagittarius". The donor requested that the money be used to build and furnish a cottage to be designated "The Gift of Sagittarius, Greenock".

Quarrier would generally accept any name for the cottage which the donor suggested, but there was one occasion where he did not approve of the choice of name. The donor of the fourth cottage, Dunbartonshire, originally wanted it to be called 'Quarrier Home'— but Quarrier would have none of it. As far as he was concerned the Homes were God's, not his. I wonder what he would feel today if he knew that the entire village had been named after him!

One of the most remarkable donations made to the Homes was from Jane Stewart, an old woman who lived in Main Street, Gorbals. On March 26, 1891, a friend of Quarrier's asked him if he would come and meet an old lady who wanted to make a contribution towards the work. Quarrier duly went to call upon Jane Stewart in her tidy little Gorbals single-end, where she told him the story of her difficult, lonely life as a servant and washerwoman. She ended by saying that she wished to give something to help the Homes work. Looking round her spartan room Quarrier naturally expected very little, but to his astonishment she rummaged about in a chest of drawers and produced a wad of bank receipts, totalling over £600! Fearing that he might be depriving the old woman of her entire life's savings, Quarrier gently asked if the gift were not too much. "Na, na, I've plenty mair, an ye'll get it a' when I dee" she replied, and pushed the bundle into his hands.

Just two days later Jane Stewart died. She left over £1,000 to the Orphan Homes of Scotland, made up of a deposit receipt for £400, savings in the bank of £200, £27 15s in cash and 55 shares in the Lancashire Insurance Company bought twenty years before and now worth over £400! All this was the thrifty accumulation of 55 years of meagre earnings as a servant and washerwoman. As a fitting tribute to this remarkable old woman, her money was used towards the provision of a new piped water-supply for the Homes.

The gifts which arrived on Quarrier's desk every day were not just for the building of cottages. The Orphan Homes were much more than a collection of houses. Behind the Central Building a training ship was erected, the *James Arthur,* a fully- rigged vessel cemented to the ground in which some 30 boys lived and worked as part of their training for a career in the merchant navy. The Homes had their own school and their own poultry farm. There was a park down by the River Gryffe with swings and see-saws, and an outdoor swimming pond in the Cattie. And down by the workshops were greenhouses to grow all kinds of vegetables for the large family, as well as stables and a coach-house.

Quarrier had the mammoth task of maintaining this extraordinary village and providing for the hundreds of men, women and children who lived and worked in it. And yet he never knew, from one day to the next, if he would have sufficient funds. Daily maintenance of the City Home and the Orphan Homes was about £40 in the early 1890's; but Quarrier was very strict about using gifts which were sent to him each day. His rule was that money could only be used for the purpose specified by the donor, so that if £10 were sent in for the Bridge of Weir Building Fund when he needed £10 for food, he could not use it. Furthermore, there was never any money comfortably gathering interest in the bank, which could be drawn on in emergencies, because Quarrier would not allow the stockpiling of funds. Every penny sent was ploughed into the work (this is still the case today), so that anyone who donated money would know that it was being used directly and effectively. For this reason Quarrier would not accept any endowments for the future maintenance of the Homes, and in 1881 he had to refuse £8,000 offered in this way for one of the cottages. He trusted completely to unsolicited gifts from generous people and his trust was not let down—the children never went hungry or cold; but often the financial year closed only just on the right side—in 1888 the balance was 11s 4½d! And many a day his diary made anxious reading:

Aug 2   Only 12 shillings today, and our wants are many
Aug 4   From Dumbarton, £100. This was needed and has greatly cheered us.

As the cottages were built, the children filled them, arriving daily from the City Home in James Morrison Street which acted as a receiving centre. Every child's case was looked into there, and the particulars taken down, before admission to Bridge of Weir. The qualifications for entry to the Orphan Homes were listed on the back of every *Narrative of Facts* :

> Bridge of Weir, Renfrewshire — Orphan boys and girls deprived of both parents, children of widows, or others with no relative able or willing to keep them, from 1 to 14 years of age, from any part of the country. Destitution is the title for admission, and there is no subscriber's line or voting paper required.

An up-to-date file was kept on every single child who was registered at the City Home, and the notes fill volume after volume. It's not known if Quarrier himself wrote the early files, but it would certainly be in keeping with his energy and the personal interest he took in every aspect of the work. But whoever wrote them, these Diaries of Admission are not just a catalogue of misery and poverty, or neglected children in their thousands; each page is a portrait of a real person. Years and years before the concept of the social worker and case-notes, William Quarrier dealt with each child as an individual, colourful personality. Reading the faded entries, beautifully hand-written on the thick, musty-smelling pages of enormous bound notebooks, is like looking at very old black-and-white photographic portraits: the sense of the past is strong and yet there is also a thrilling depth and immediacy. Here are a few of the entries from the volume of 1890 to 1891:

HUNTER, ROBERT

1890

Dec. 5   Robert says he is 14 past.
He is sent here by Charity Organistaion Society to whom he was sent by a Dr. at Western Infirmary Dispensary where he went on account of broken out head. Dr. says it is caused by neglect and quite curable. His story is that he walked from Linlithgow where he lived for some time but has been wandering all about since his father left 18 mos. ago. He heard father Wm., a brassfinisher, had gone to America. Mother dead 4 years. He is taken meantime and C.O.S. will make enquiry. He can't read.

1891

Jan. 28   Dismissed on this date and fare paid to Linlithgow where he says he can find some friends. Letter of enquiry sent by C.O.S. was returned so that he is evidently not truthful. As collection box in hall was broken open a few nights ago while he was door-boy (there was no money in it) and he had been spending money of which he could not give very satisfactory account his honesty was doubted and as nothing could be found out about his friends the above course was thought best.

In the house he was quiet, obliging and well-behaved.

STEVENSON, DUNCAN

1890

Nov. 27   Duncan born 7 July 1881 at 41 Hospital St. Gorbals. He seems a poor "subject". He wants an eye, has a lisp and is only on 6th book. He had measles and whooping cough. Father Robert Gillespie Stevenson a carter, 25 N. Coburg St., is unable to work with chronic Bronchitis and his wife Eliz. M.S. Murray is a cripple from paralysis so that they purpose going into Poor House to see whether or not they regain strength sufficient to do some work. Father signs emigration form (X).

Letter of recommendation from Wm. Gilford, 114 Hospital St., who has known them for 4 years.

Given back to father who for some reason known to himself regretted leaving him here.

WALLACE, GEORGE

1890

Dec. 13   George is said to be 16 years of age.

He had hip-joint disease and in consequence uses a crutch. He does not look strong. On account of his health and also as parents could afford to give him a light job he has not been at work but having musical talent he was being taught violin-playing with view of making it a profession. As circumstances have changed he wishes to earn a living by tailoring or brush-making and although rather old not to have been at work he seems a decent lad and promises to do as wanted.

Parents dead. Mother died in June and since then a brother Wm., a druggist living at 94 Main St Rutherglen, has kept him but can't continue as he has broken down in health, and is being treated for chest disease in Western Infirmary — Koch treatment — and has been idle 5 months. Wm. is married. He brings Geo. here.

1896

Aug. 21   To lodgings. His apprenticeship as a tailor with David Angus, York St., is finished. He is still very delicate.

1897

Jan.   Married to Effie Kin(?)

1907

Feb. 17   George died this date of consumption.

What happened to all those thousands of children whose lives appear briefly on the pages of the Diaries of Admissions? I could read through the entries for hours, just wondering and imagining.

After registration at the City Home it was decided where the child should be sent—either to one of the Brigades, or perhaps to the Working Lads' Home or to Bridge of Weir. At Bridge of Weir a child would be placed in a cottage with 30 or more other boys or girls. The daily routine was necessarily strictly governed, with rising-time, meals, chores and family worship an unchanging part of the controlled time-table. But Quarrier always aimed to have individuality and family-feeling as much as possible among the children; there were no uniforms or any kind of strange garb which would brand the children as orphans and Homes boys and girls. The ages in each cottage ranged from toddlers upwards, and Quarrier hoped that this, too, would foster a sense of friendship and family.

Each cottage marched to school in the morning in an orderly group. Elementary education was given, as well as sewing classes for the girls. By the 1890's the Education (Scotland) Act of 1872 was well in force and school attendance between the ages of 5 and 13 was compulsory, although it would still be many years before all parents did send their children to school. Once his children were past school age, Quarrier saw to it that they received some sort of training for a trade. The boys could be apprenticed to the joiners, printers, carpenters and shoemakers who worked in the village and the girls trained for domestic service in the laundry and sewing rooms, as well as by helping with the running of the cottage. This was central to Quarrier's conviction that what these children needed was not just to be brought up in home-like surroundings, but also to be trained to find their own way honestly and successfully in life afterwards, and not be thrown back on the mercy of street and parish.

By 1897 there were 37 cottages housing over 900 children in the Orphan Homes. Since 1878 52 buildings had been constructed and thousands of children had been helped. And still the money arrived each day, and still the work expanded. But it was not always plain sailing at Bridge of Weir, and Quarrier, who was an uncompromising man, incurred criticism from various quarters about the way he ran things. On one occasion the Catholic community of Glasgow accused him of proselytism and of withholding children whose parents or relatives were now in a position to look after them and wanted them back. He went to court over the matter and was completely exonerated; but there were others to question his firm and sometimes overbearing methods. The *Glasgow Herald,* always quick to criticise his work, claimed that he had too much power over an organisation which received its funds entirely from the public, and declared that the Homes should be run by a committee.

One of the biggest wrangles Quarrier was involved in was over the paying of rates to the Renfrewshire County Council. The dispute began in 1896 and dragged on for more than six years. These were difficult times for Quarrier and the work of the Homes. When the row broke out other matters were also causing concern: an outbreak of Scarlatina (a mild form of Scarlet Fever) among the children, and the failure of Quarrier's own health later that year due to the kidney trouble which was to dog him for years. In addition, the Homes had been taken to court by the proprietor of some neighbouring farm because of a drainage problem for which he blamed Quarrier. And the following year, 1897, emigration to Canada was stopped because of legislation passed in Ontario which Quarrier took exception to.

So amid all this, an argument with Renfrewshire County Council was the last thing Quarrier needed. For the past 16 years the Orphan Homes had not paid any rates since they came under the 1869 "Sunday and Ragged School Act" which exempted from such taxation "institutions for the gratuitous education of children and young persons of the poorest classes, without any pecuniary benefit being derived therefrom by the teacher". The nineteenth century had seen many such Ragged Schools spring up all over Britain, following the example of John Pounds, a Portsmouth cobbler, who in 1818 held classes in the 3 Rs for the waifs and orphans around the docks there. Dr. Guthrie of Edinburgh published his *Plea for Ragged Schools* in 1847 and set up the city's first premises where the children of poor people could go to learn reading and writing and the basic skills of some trade, like shoemaking, as well as receiving free meals.

On a larger scale, this was what Quarrier was offering in the Orphan Homes and he considered the Homes very much a Ragged School.

Registered for Transmission Abroad.

The Bailie.

"MY CONSCIENCE!"

No. 414. Glasgow, Wednesday, September 22nd, 1880. Price 1d

MEN YOU KNOW—No. 414.

TO seek the good of our fellow-men is, as we
all know, the most elevated of human pur-
suits. The profession of a philanthropist enables
you, to use a phrase which used to be commoner
a couple of decades ago than it is to-day, to
make the best of both worlds. You not only
get unlimited credit in this life by your deeds,
but their savour lasts even unto the life which
is to come. Philanthropists, to be sure, are
seldom to be reckoned among the most likeable
of mortals. If his biographers may be believed,
John Howard was a harsh father and an indif-
ferent friend. History, indeed, is generally
silent as to the individual excellencies of people
of the Howard class. Before you can set up as
a philanthropist, you must not only be possessed
by a notion that the people round about you are
a poor lot, but that you yourself are a person of
pre-eminent virtue. It would be impossible to
preserve the position of a philanthropist were
you to come down from your pedestal, even for
a day, and believe that you were no more than
as are those whom you have set yourself to suc-
cour and save. It is one thing, however, to watch
the weaknesses of philanthropists—their inor-
dinate vanity, their dislike of opposition, the
bitterness they display toward all who take up
a like *role* with themselves—and another to con-
temn the work they have set themselves to do.
Our friend WILLIAM QUARRIER, for instance,
is one of the purest-minded and most earnest
men living. His whole life is devoted to a noble
end, and it may be questioned whether any other
single individual has really effected more good
in this city of ours during the last ten years than
that which has resulted from his individual
efforts. Personally, however, Mr QUARRIER is
susceptible of a large degree of improvement.

VOL. XVI.

He is imperious beyond everything. No rival
is allowed to approach within bowing distance
even of his throne. He simply will not tolerate
criticism. Whatever savours of mirth or gaiety
finds in him a sworn foe. To people, besides,
whose ideas are of the humbler sort, he seems to
live and move in an atmosphere of absolute and
even outrageous irreverence. He has so accus-
tomed himself to regard Providence as a species
of adjunct to his schemes for ameliorating the
condition of our city Arabs, that his addresses
to the Higher Powers are couched in the form of
command rather than of supplication. The
BAILIE respects Mr QUARRIER with an ex-
ceeding great respect; but if some measure
of sweetness—it were too much to ask for
light—were mingled with the unwearied devo-
tion, the unselfish effort which marks his every-
day work, how worthy he would be of liking
as well as admiration. He counts it gain to
spend and be spent in the cause of the needy
and the suffering; but the narrowness of his
view, the intensity of his egotism, give serious
cause for annoyance to the more earnest among
us and supply those of an irreverent temper
with material for amusement, and occasionally
for even scoffing and laughter. Mr QUARRIER'S
first public efforts were made in connection with
the shoe black brigade, the members of which
were boarded, educated, and cared for under his
supervision. The main work of his life, however, has been the erection of the Orphan Cottage Homes of Scotland at Bridge of Weir.
These were started some eight years ago, and
to-day forty acres of ground, and handsome cottages and villas capable of accommodating from
two hundred to three hundred children, show a
splendid result of Mr QUARRIER'S labours. Besides the Bridge of Weir Institution, Mr QUAR-
RIER has started and superintend a boys' and
girls' home at Cessnock House, near Govan; and

---

*An extract from "The Bailie" a publication which was well known for its sharp
comments on leading personalities of the day (Reproduced by Courtesy of THE MITCHELL LIBRARY)*

ATTEMPT GREAT THINGS FOR GOD: EXPECT GREAT THINGS FROM HIM.

H. T., a Physical Wreck through want and neglect,
as received, 1886

The Narrative of Facts frequently carried this kind of Before and After illustration
of the children who came to Bridge of Weir

But suddenly, out of the blue, in 1896 the County Council of Renfrewshire announced its intention to claim back-rates and to start taxing the Homes in the normal fashion. Quarrier was very angry and refused to pay. The whole system at Bridge of Weir, he said, was and always had been based on the Ragged School—the teachers at the school received no guaranteed salary, all the workers were volunteers, and the sole source of funds was donations. The Homes themselves made no demands on the local council since they had their own water supply, their own bakery and handymen, and no claim was made on the Kilmacolm School Board for assistance in educating the children.

The matter went to the Court of Session, but the decision went against Quarrier. The judge pronounced, finely, that the Orphan Homes of Scotland were "a large and very highly developed Ragged School", therefore more than a Ragged School, therefore liable for normal rating. The *Narrative of Facts* of 1898 seethes with Quarrier's indignation at the decision:

> The Ragged and Sunday Schools Act gives provision for holding meetings or classes, and doing other work of a voluntary kind; and this is what we contend for, that the whole concern is for the gratuitous education and feeding of the hungry, which this Act does not prohibit being done. Who can conceive of a child being educated who has no home to live in, and no moral surroundings: the thing is out of reason. Every Ragged School from the first one of John Pounds the cobbler, down to the present day, has not withheld food as well as lodging for the homeless; and because we do our work better are we not to have the benefit of all that the law can do for us?

Quarrier appealed, but to no avail, and the following year he was ordered to pay five years of back-rates amounting to £800, £300 for the legal expenses of the Council, and his own expenses of £600.

This was galling enough; but then the Parish Council of Kilmacolm saw their chance and stepped in with a demand for four years of parish and school back-rates! And yet the School Board of Kilmacolm had never made any provision for the education of the Orphan Homes' children, let alone given assistance over the past four years. Furthermore, the Board would not assure Quarrier that if he paid the rates they would undertake the future education of his children. At a loss to understand their attitude, and incensed at the way in which he and his children were being treated, Quarrier declared war on the Kilmacolm Board. His strategy was typically bold and direct. One morning in April he marched the two miles along the road from the Homes to Kilmacolm at the head of a vast army of 800 of his children, column upon column of them, carrying banners and flanked by their cottage parents. Quarrier led his troops straight to Kilmacolm School where an irate member of the Board refused him admission. Undeterred, Quarrier turned to address the children and the interested crowd which had gathered. In a loud voice he explained the purpose of the protest—to draw attention to the Board's unfair and disgraceful actions—and finished with a formal demand that the School Board fulfill its responsibilities and educate his children. Then William Quarrier turned on his heel and marched back home, closely followed by his 800 children.

It was a dramatic gesture which must have caused the Board acute embarrassment, but even so, it was several years before the dispute was finally resolved. Just before his death in 1903 Quarrier arranged a meeting with the Board, and as a result of this they took over responsibility for the education of the Homes children soon afterwards. It took a long time, but in the end Quarrier did win his battle for his children.

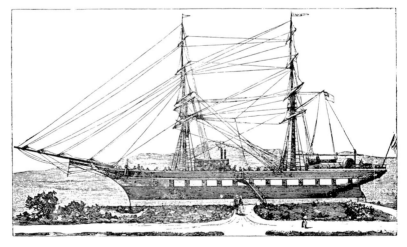

The "James Arthur" training ship

CHAPTER FIVE

The Golden Bridge

A rescue home must be continuously gathering in fresh inmates, else in a single generation it would be compelled to close its doors and write in the face of new applicants 'No admission'. But to secure the open door in front, it must maintain its exit door in the rear.*

So said Dr. Thomas Barnardo to his trustees one day in the late 1870s as he outlined his plans for the emigration of English children to Canada. Canada, the new world, the infant country with great open spaces and untapped natural resources, was to be the "exit door" for the thousands of pauper and orphaned children Barnardo had been rescuing from London's teeming streets. His boast was that no destitute child would ever be refused admission to his boys' home in Stepney or his girls' cottages in Barkingside; but this inevitably meant a constant stream of children to his door, and to cope with the increasing numbers Barnardo now began to look across the Atlantic to the farms and homesteads of Ontario, Quebec and Manitoba, where thousands of British children had already been settled by various charitable organisations. Those who sent the children spoke of a new life for them, a chance for a new future far away from the grime, overcrowding and poverty of Britain's industrial cities. They saw emigration as advantageous to the child, good for Canada — an

*This statement by Dr Barnardo is taken from Kenneth Bagnell's book, *The Little Immigrants* (Macmillan of Canada, 1980) p140, which has also provided much of the background for this chapter.

expanding country which desperately needed labour and settlers —
and an ideal way of easing the burden of Britain's poor and homeless
children.

It had all been started by an Englishwoman called Maria Susan Rye,
a zealous, determined character who worked among the poor people
of London. In 1868 she went to Canada and bought an old jail on the
outskirts of a small town called Niagara-on-the-Lake which lay at the
mouth of the River Niagara at Lake Ontario. The jail was gutted and
refurbished, and in October, 1869, Maria Rye took 68 children from
Liverpool and London to Montreal on the S.S *Hibernian*. The
children, from the workhouses of London and an industrial school in
Liverpool, were of all ages, the youngest (nine and under) bound for
adoption, and the older ones to be indentured as farm hands or
domestics.

Maria Rye was followed just a few months later by Annie
Macpherson, the tireless Scots philanthropist who came to work in
London in 1865 and who encouraged William Quarrier to go ahead
with his plan for a children's Home in Renfrew Lane. She, like
Barnardo after her, saw emigration as a positive solution to the
problem of London's overcrowded, poverty-ridden streets. She
proclaimed her conviction in a stirring pamphlet written in 1869:

> We who labour here are tired of relieving misery from hand to mouth, and also
> heartsick of seeing hundreds of families pining away for want of work, when over
> on the shores of Ontario the cry is heard, 'Come over and we will help you'...We
> are waiting to seek out the worthy not yet on the parish list, but who soon must
> be; we will see to their being properly started on the Canadian shores if you will
> give us the power to make a golden bridge across the Atlantic.

In the spring of 1870 Annie Macpherson took 100 boys from her
own rescue homes, the workhouse and the reformatories in London,
to Ontario. There the townspeople of Belleville, a town on Lake
Ontario, gave her a large house, rent-free, called Marchmount, to
which she could send children for distribution to farms and homesteads throughout the province. As the work expanded and Annie
Macpherson brought more and more children, she acquired other
such homes all over Ontario. The golden bridge was now well and
truly opened for traffic. Nearly 100,000 children from all over Britain

A typical Canadian farmstead to which British Homes Children were so often sent
(Reproduced by Courtesy of Barnardo's)

William Quarrier onboard ship with a party of girls bound for Canada (Reproduced from Urquhart's "The Life-Story of William Quarrier")

would cross it during the period from 1870 to the early 1930s — over 30,000 of them sent by Thomas Barnardo alone.

Dr. Barnardo's first party of 51 boys made the journey to Canada in 1882. By that time William Quarrier had been sending children for ten years. From the first he recognised emigration as an important factor in his work for Scotland's orphans, and when he met Annie Macpherson they agreed that he would send the children from his Renfrew Lane Home to Canada under her auspices. For Quarrier, emigration was not just a convenient means of clearing Glasgow's streets of waifs and strays; of course, it was clear that his Glasgow Homes had limited accommodation and training facilities for the children and that emigration was essential if more and more were to be rescued, but Quarrier also firmly believed that emigration was in the best interests of his children and that Canada was truly the land of opportunity, where boys and girls could make a good future for themselves in a new, eager country which needed them. His children would be following the route taken by thousands of pioneers and settlers before them, not least their Scottish ancestors. After the Jacobite Rebellion in 1745 and the break-up of the clan system, wave upon wave of Highlanders broke on the distant shores of eastern Canada. They settled in Quebec, Ontario, Cape Breton and right across to British Columbia, sharing the vast unexplored land with peoples from all over the world.

Ontario was by far the most popular province and it was to this area that Quarrier sent his first band of children on July 2, 1872. The group consisted of 35 boys from the Cessnock Home and 29 other children from orphanages in Maryhill and Edinburgh, all under the charge of Quarrier's friend the Rev. Stobo, and Miss Bryson, one of the teachers at Renfrew Lane. Their ship, the *St. David* was one of the Allan Line steamers, identified by their red, white and black funnels, which made regular voyages from Glasgow to Canada and America. On the morning of departure, Quarrier's boys were marched from Cessnock to the Broomielaw, their trunks going on ahead by horse and cart. At the dockside all was activity and bustle as people gathered to see off the ship, many of them friends and relatives of the children. Quarrier stood among the excited, chattering boys as their

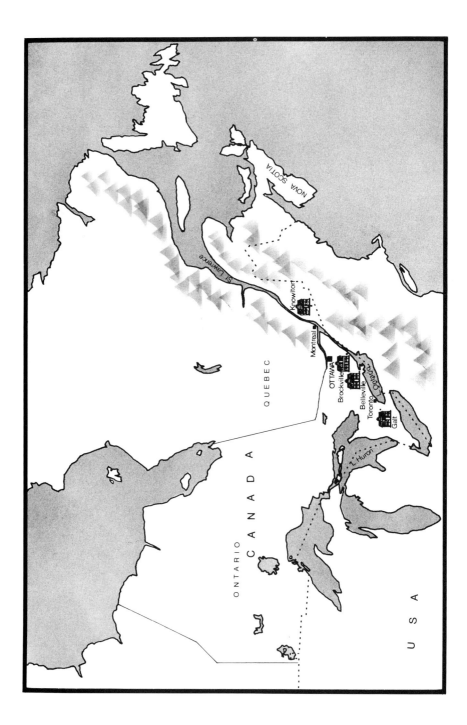

luggage was loaded onto the ship, each trunk stamped with the boy's initials and containing among other things, one cloth and two linen suits, four shirts, four pairs of socks, a box of collars, writing material and a pair of strong boots. The cost of all this and one-way passage to Quebec— just £10. Quarrier also provided his boys with one or two other items to kit them out for their new lives — a reference Bible, a copy of *Pilgrim's Progress* and a pocket knife. All good equipment for the young pioneer. At last, farewells were said, the ship's whistle on the great funnel sounded and the *St. David* cast off.

Looking after 64 excited children of all ages for sixteen days in the middle of the Atlantic was not without its difficulties, and the Rev. Stobo's journal is full of vivid little details of life on board:

> It is difficult to prevent things going astray on board ship, and some people allow things strange to them to stick to them, to others' loss and discomfort... Of course. boys cannot be made girls, they will be boisterous and romping, and full of fun, and it s no use trying to coop them up in a corner.

The ship steamed up the St. Lawrence River on July 17 and arrived in Quebec at noon the following day. From there the whole party went by train to Montreal and then east to one of Annie Macpherson's distribution homes in the little township of Knowlton. Brome Hall, a converted public house, was run by a Miss Barbour, and the Rev. Stobo stayed just long enough to hand over into her care some of his charges to be sent to homes in this south-eastern corner of Quebec. Then he was off again, this time west to Annie Macpherson's main home, Marchmount, in Belleville. This home was later put in the charge of one of Annie Macpherson's closest friends, Ellen Agnes Bilbrough, and used exclusively for Quarrier's children until 1887 when Quarrier built a brand new home in Brockville, a little further up the St. Lawrence River. Marchmount home distributed children all over central Canada and to farmsteads for 200 miles in all directions, some of them extremely isolated.

The Rev. Stobo's last port of call was the town of Galt, named after the Scottish novelist John Galt, which lay south west of Lake Ontario. He delivered more children there, this time to Blair Athole, a farm just outside the town which served as another of Annie Macpherson's distribution homes. In all, the Rev. Stobo spent six weeks in Canada

T.V.

E₂

and travelled over 3,500 miles by pony-trap, wagon and train, delivering his precious cargo of children. He accompanied some of them all the way to their new homes in outlying districts and this often meant long, uncomfortable journeys on poor roads.

Ontario in the 1870s was, like most of the rest of Canada, a rural province. Of a populaton of 3,500,000 in Canada in 1871, only about 12% lived in cities and towns, and only twenty towns had more than 5,000 inhabitants. Montreal, with 107,000 inhabitants, Quebec with 60,000 and Toronto with 57,000 were the three most concentrated areas of population in the entire country. And what of the vast open countryside that was the rest of Canada? Well, nothing could have been more different to the eyes and experience of a child born and raised on the dirty, crowded streets of nineteenth century Glasgow. To the children Quarrier sent over to Canada, Ontario would have seemed an almost unrecognisable world: small hamlets and tiny communities spread over empty miles instead of high tenements stacked against one another and lining the streets; acres of wheat fields and miles of grasslands instead of teeming thoroughfares. A child sent to a remote farm in Ontario might be many miles from his nearest neighbour and would certainly have to traverse a considerable distance to attend school. The only regular social gathering he would encounter would probably be weekly church attendance.

Everything must have looked different, smelt different and sounded different. Vast blue skies and burning sun in the summer months, and then sub-zero winter temperatures and quantities of snow such as were never seen in the Gallowgate! Many a child would have encountered a cow for the first time in his life—and how strange the farm with all its animals and open spaces would smell! And how would the wind rushing across the fields and through the trees sound to a young girl in bed at night who had spent most of her life amid the bustle and clamour of Glasgow's streets?

However unfamiliar and strange Canada seemed to these girls and boys, they would have had little time to cry. They were there to work; those under twelve were adopted and worked as part of the family for their board and keep; the older children were indentured and paid a small wage which went into a savings account to be given to them

The Golden Bridge
MISS BILBROUGH'S HOME, CANADA.

Marchmont Home, Belleville, Ontario, 24th Oct., 1879.

DEAR FRIENDS,—It is with feelings of deep gratitude, I sit down to write my usual contribution to our Annual Report, knowing how much interest is taken by you in the well doing of the children sent out from Scotland.

Reproduced from the 1879 Narrative of Facts

when they left their employer. In the months before a party of children arrived, those in charge at the Canadian end—Miss Bilbrough and later Quarrier's daughter, Agnes, and her husband, James Burges—advertised through churches, in local newspapers and Christian and missionary circles, for those farmers either interested in adopting a "Scotch child" or taking one on as a farm hand. Agnes Bilbrough described in her booklet *British Children in Canadian Homes* the pains which were taken to make sure of the suitability of each home, but all the process seems to have involved was talking to the applicant, asking round the neighbours and gaining a good word from the local minister. It appears from Miss Bilbrough's account that a farmer who arrived on the doorstep to pick out a child simply needed to produce a reference, sign a few papers and take the child away.

But whatever the shortcomings in the selection of homes, Agnes Bilbrough did keep a careful note of each child and where he or she

57

went. All the children were registered and every applicant had to sign a Form of Indenture for a child of twelve or over:

This indenture, made this ....day of .... (Pursuant to Order in Council bearing date 9th of December, 1879, authorising Marchmount Home to exercise the powers granted under sec. 19 of cap. 135, RSO) is entered into between Ellen Agnes Billbrough, Marchmount, guardian of .... and Mr. .... respecting .... To receive 4 dollars per month for the first year, increasing annually. To attend Church and Sunday School regularly. Also day school four months in the year. Should it be necessary in any case for the child to be returned to the Home, notice of this must be sent a fortnight beforehand. The clothes must also be sent back in good condition, and the same number. Employers are requested to see that the children write occasionally to their friends; also that they communicate with us in event of sickness. An accurate account to be kept by employer of the wages spent in child's clothing etc. The account to be balanced each year, and said balance to be deposited in Savings Bank, or otherwise laid out to child's advantage. Persons taking these children cannot transfer them to others, but are at liberty to return them to the Home if they do not suit, while we, on our part, reserve the right of removing any child if we see fit, or on these conditions not being fulfilled.

Anyone who adopted a child under twelve had to sign a form along the same lines, but instead of wages the child was to receive "good clothing and schooling and to be treated as one of the family".

Annual visits by representatives of the Home were really the only way to check that things were well with the child and that the terms of agreement were being carried out properly. Word of trouble, however, might travel along the grapevine of church circles and neighbours' stories, and if the Home suspected anything was wrong they would send out the Visitor. The Visitor tried to do the job conscientiously but time, distance and numbers made it a very hard task. The numbers of children sent over from Quarrier's homes in Glasgow increased steadily, especially after the opening of the Homes at Bridge of Weir. 35 boys were sent out in the first year, 1872, 66 the following year, 103 in 1879 and in 1881 two separate parties—50 boys in March and 68 girls in May. After this, two parties were sent out every year and in 1885 there was even a third exodus—in all, a total of 339 children went to Canada in that year alone. To cope with the rising numbers, in 1887 Quarrier built his new distribution home, solely for his children, in a little town called Brockville. It was called

Fairknowe Home and it still stands in the town today, as an apartment block. The records of the 2,000 children already in the country were transferred to the new home, and Quarrier's daughter and her husband went out to run the operation.

They had a huge task. Quarrier's children were spread over a vast area that stretched from the eastern shores of Lake Huron right across to Montreal and beyond, and from Lake Ontario in the south to the borders of Quebec. James Burges' brother, Alexander, was Fairknowe's principal resident Visitor and he spent virtually the whole year trekking through the countryside to outlying farms, in all weathers, checking up on the children. His report of 1892, by which time his visiting role listed some 3,000 names (although many of these would be grown-up Quarrier's boys and girls), gives some idea of the travelling which was involved:

> Last fall I drove as far west as Belleville, taking Wolfe Island, Amherst Island, and Prince Edward County on my way west, and visiting the northern part of the counties on my return. As the roads were heavy, it was anything but agreeable work. After New Year I went through all Western Ontario, getting back in time to meet the party of boys. During summer I got over a good deal of ground, although the weather was exceedingly warm, and we had a number of unusually severe storms... During the year we have visited over 2,000 of the children.

Generally Fairknowe was well satisfied with its children and their new lives—the Burgeses always maintained that about 95% of them did well and only a very small percentage ran off, or were a source of trouble or annoyance. Quarrier did not draw his children straight from reformatory schools or out of the poorhouse as did people like Maria Rye in England, and he insisted that they were not simply decanted from Glasgow's streets into the homesteads of Ontario, but received training at home beforehand. In the early days this could not have been much more than being cleaned up and taught a little reading and writing and some table manners, for Cessnock and Renfield Homes were really just transit homes—children would be admitted and packed off to Canada within months. However, once the Homes at Bridge of Weir were opened it was possible to train the children for longer periods and prepare them a little for their new lives. As far

The Girls' Party of 1897 at Fairknowe Home. William Quarrier and his wife are standing in the middle of the second row from the back

as he could help it, Quarrier did not send wild or unruly children or those likely to revert to street habits of stealing or roughness, and he believed he was supplying Canada with good future citizens.

Ironically, it was this that aroused a degree of hostile criticism at home. Some sections of Scottish business and industry complained that such mass emigration of Scotland's young was draining the future labour market; Quarrier's confident reply was that it wasn't the labour market he was reducing but a future crime market of children abandoned to the streets, and that by taking them in at an early age, training them up and sending them to new lives in Canada he was doing the poorhouse, the rate-payers, the citizens and the children a favour.

But the British emigration movement faced far more serious and disturbing criticism than this. Three years after Quarrier sent his first party of boys to Ontario, a report was published in England which exposed serious shortcomings in some of the British agencies for child emigration. The report was written by Andrew Doyle, a 65-year-old lawyer and former inspector of the London Poor Law Board. The Local Government Board, who had taken over the work of the Poor Law Board, decided in 1874 that an investigation should be made of the various British emigration bodies. The scheme had been running for five years now, and the Board had supplied it with hundreds of children from England's workhouses and reformatories. They formed a considerable proportion of the 2,000-odd boys and girls now scattered across Canada from Nova Scotia to Manitoba. Rumours had reached the Board which caused them anxiety about the welfare of some of the children and so, in the spring of 1874, they sent out Andrew Doyle to investigate.

His findings were far from reassuring. He spent six months travelling round the country, visiting first the distribution homes of Maria Rye and Annie Macpherson and then as many of the children as he could. He questioned Miss Rye and Miss Macpherson and all their helpers, inquiring into everything from finances to the sleeping arrangements for the children coming into their homes. And his conclusion was that, although both Maria Rye and Annie Macpherson were led by the best and most sincere motives, their respective organisations were badly run along the whole line, from the initial selection of children to their placing out in Canadian farms.

One of his main worries was that little or no distinction was made in the choosing of the children from the workhouses between paupers and waifs who were there through no fault of their own, and the hardened street arabs, many of them thieves and semi-criminals from an early age. Children were simply lifted from the workhouses, wrote Andrew Doyle, the good apples with the bad, and many a farmer ended up receiving an unruly thief for a farm hand, which lent discredit to the whole movement.

Andrew Doyle also criticised the forms of indenture which each applicant had to sign. These were not stringent enough to ensure the child's well-being, and prospective households were not inspected properly beforehand. On the subject of inspection and visiting, Doyle had his most hard-hitting remarks to make, though here he carefully distinguished between Annie Macpherson's operation and Maria Rye's. He was absolutely appalled by the lack of any proper supervision of Maria Rye's children once they had been taken off her hands. She didn't even keep records, so that she had no idea of what happened to most of them—they could have been ill-treated and left their guardian or employer, and she would have known nothing about it. Doyle was less severe on Annie Macpherson and he had nothing but praise for Agnes Bilbrough. "The liberal and unostentatious way", he wrote, "in which that lady devotes the rare gifts with which she is endowed to the fulfillment of very onerous duties is beyond all praise". He recognised that Annie Macpherson did have a system of visiting which was carried out as faithfully as possible, but it was imperfect; there were simply too many children, they were too far afield and one annual visit was not enough.

Amazingly, Andrew Doyle's report and his call for a much more carefully-planned and regulated emigration system was almost totally ignored in Canada. It was widely reported in the British press and demands were made for a halt to the movement until things had been put right. But in Canada most people simply refused to believe the report and the supporters of Maria Rye, who did not want to see their source of labour disappear, poured scorn on Doyle and his findings.

Some years later, though, public opinion in Canada began to change. Although farmers always remained in favour of the British children, the 1880s saw many Canadians turn against immigration. During the late 1870s and mid-1880s Canada suffered periodic bouts of economic depression and the anxieties and frustrations of working men became focussed, not unnaturally, on the foreign workforce flooding the country. British children became the target for much criticism and there was resentment from the Canadian Trades and Labour Council, led by the trade unionist D. J. O'Donaghue, who said that they were a source of cheap labour which deprived the Canadian working man of a job. In addition, the very occasional court case involving a "Home Boy" and (generally unfounded) stories of assaults by such boys on their masters fuelled fears that Canada was becoming the dumping ground for the depraved and criminal elements of Britain's slums. "Canada wants increased population" wrote the *Globe* in 1884, "but she would not on that account thank any country for landing the inmates of its prisons and poor-houses on her shores".

In 1896 the case of a Barnardo boy, George Green, fanned the flames of controversy still higher. This poor boy was found dead, and in the most appalling state of filth and disease, at the farm of Miss Helen Findlay in Owen Sound, Ontario. According to the coroner, the boy died as a result of neglect, starvation and violence. During the trial of Miss Findlay for manslaughter it emerged that she had often been seen by neighbours physically abusing George—kicking him, hitting him with the handle of an axe and poking him with a pitchfork. But what caused the greatest furore in the press, far more than the charges of assault (which Miss Findlay denied), were other medical reports on George Green which claimed that he was physically extremely defective, had bad eyesight and had been suffering from a tuberculosis-related condition. In fact, announced the doctors who performed the second autopsy, George Green was a weak physical specimen to start with.

The Canadian press leapt upon this revelation and set up a clamour of invective against the practice of sending such diseased young people to infect their country and declared that the case exposed once and for all the weakness of the medical examinations of these British

Fairknowe Home, Brockville, which Quarrier had built in 1887

children coming into the country. Nobody seemed to think it worthwhile pointing out that the case of George Green also indicated the chilling possibility of the ill-treatment of other children abandoned to isolated farms and left to the mercy of their employers.

But one man did fear the possibility that there were many George Greens all over Canada. He was John Kelso, the founding President of the Toronto branch of the Children's Aid Society and the Superintendent of Neglected Children in Ontario. He prepared 'A Special Report on the Immigration of British Children' in 1897 in which he urged the regulation of the work, the official inspection of all emigration organistaions and the tightening up of visiting and inspection of children.

By this time there were nearly 40,000 British children in Canada, and 28,945 of them were on farms in Ontario. The federal government of Ontario realised that something had to be done to improve and control the traffic in children, to protect them from possible cruelty and suffering and to safeguard Canada from an influx of undesirables. So in March, 1897, Ontario passed an "Act to Regulate the Immigration into Ontario of Certain Classes of Children", which was designed to place Homes children under official control from the moment they stepped off the boat until the age of 18. Each Home had to apply for a licence and keep an up-to-date account of the character, movements and habits of every child in its hands.

Thus Ontario tried to keep track of all the British children within its borders. But William Quarrier was very angry at the new legislation. **His** children had never been complained about or diseased, or in trouble with the law, so why should he have to submit to all this new red tape and officialdom? He saw the act as interfering with his work and could see no justification for it. What irritated him most of all was that his work, far from being criticised, had always been praised by the government in Ontario; John Kelso had always maintained that Quarrier's organisation was well-run, as had the premier, Arthur Hardy, who wrote personally to Quarrier in 1897 to explain the need for the Act, and to reiterate that it in no way reflected badly on Quarrier's work. But Quarrier would not be appeased. The letter only made the new law appear more unfair and unnecessary for his children and he would have none of it. He refused to see that there were very many other people involved in the matter who were not carrying out their work as conscientiously as he, and that this legislation was an attempt to protect *their* children. One-man show that he was, Quarrier would not see that there could not be one law for him and a different one for everyone else. He remained stubborn and unco-operative; if he couldn't send children to Ontario exactly as he had been sending them before, he just wouldn't send any more.

So that year at Bridge of Weir there was no sound of hammering in the workshops where the trunks for Canada were made; no one went round the cottages making up lists of young emigrants and no bookings were made with the Allan Line. It seemed that the gates of the Orphan Homes of Scotland would remain firmly shut in the direction of Canada. But they did open again—the traffic of Quarrier's children across the golden bridge was not over yet.

CHAPTER SIX

Real Lonesome

ATHENS IS A SMALL town in eastern Ontario. It lies 15 miles north of Brockville where William Quarrier built Fairknowe Home. The Home is now an apartment block but there is at least one man in neighbouring Athens who remembers it as it used to be when it was the receiving centre for thousands of children sent to Canada from the Orphan Homes of Scotland. That man is the retired police chief of Athens, Alexander Thomson MacLean, known to the town as "Scotty" MacLean. He came out to Canada in 1930 as one of a party of boys from Bridge of Weir, worked on farms in Ontario until the War broke out and then joined the Canadian Army. After demobilization he came to Athens and joined the police force, becoming its police chief in 1962.

Scotty is just one of thousands of men and women living all over Canada who originate from the Orphan Homes at Bridge of Weir. Quarrier stopped sending children in 1897 after the passing of the Ontario Act but emigration was begun again in 1904, the year after the founder died. His daughters and son-in-law, Pastor David Findlay, decided that the Act was not a hindrance, as Quarrier had obstinately maintained, and in fact afforded much better protection and safeguards for the children. The Act ensured that each child's new home would be inspected at least once a year by an independent government official, as well as by representatives of the various emigration agencies. There were to be rigorous medical examinations

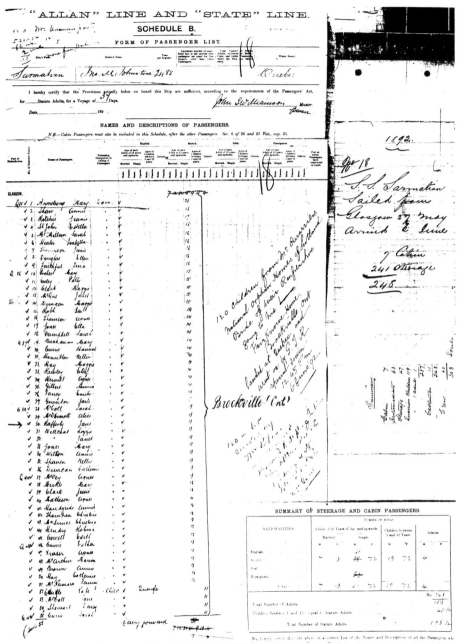

Extract from the Passenger List of the S.S. SARMATIAN (Courtesy of the Public Archives of Canada). The top half of the hand-written section reads "120 children from Mr. Quarrier's National Orphan Homes of Scotland, Bridge of Weir, Renfrewshire, going to his Fairknowe Home, Brockville, Ont. Landed at Quebec and went on by G.(?) I.R. special train 12.45 p.m. 6 June '92"

for every child instead of the cursory inspection on arrival in Canada. In later years officials from the Canadian government interviewed prospective emigrants in their Home in Britain, and no one who failed that test was allowed to go.

Efforts were also made to tighten up the regulations regarding the schooling of the children in Canada. Before 1897 potential employers and guardians had merely to promise that the child would attend school for a few months in the year, but the Canadian authorities gradually became stricter about this. Soon every child of school age had to attend school for the full 9 months in the year—not just for a few months in the winter when there was less to do around the farm. This made farmers less willing to take on children under school age, since it meant an extra mouth to feed in return for only limited help with the farm work. Things had changed since the pioneering 1870s and 1880s when Quarrier first sent children to Ontario; farming was becoming a serious business in the rapidly expanding and increasingly mechanised Canada of the early 1900s, and farmers wanted as much return for their money as they could get. In 1909 the average age of the boys and girls from the Orphan Homes was 13.3 and 12.8 and by 1912 the *Narrative of Facts* was reporting lessening demand for those under 14. This was in striking contrast to the pre-1897 situation. Earlier issues of the *Narrative of Facts* would often carry photographs of the girls and boys on board ship, all neatly posed in rows on deck, the tallest at the back and the tiny mites in front, peering uncertainly over their high collars and almost drowned in their starched frocks. In 1892 Quarrier accompanied more than 120 children to Quebec; according to the shipping list nearly half the children on that voyage were under 11. Seven were 8-year-olds, ten were 7, there were six 6-year-olds and a little brother and sister of just 5. Sending such young children was out of the question when emigration resumed; not only was there less demand for them, but there was still a good deal of opposition to the movement and people concerned for the welfare of the children, on both sides of the Atlantic, continued to press for stricter controls. As a result the British government ruled in 1924 that no child under 14 could be sent to work in Canada.

So things were changing on the emigration front by the time Pastor

Findlay decided it should be started again. But the same preparations had to be made. Once again, for weeks before the twice-yearly departure of the children, the Homes were a hive of activity. There were lists of names to be drawn up, trunks to be constructed, medical tests to be passed. On the evening before departure a service was held in Mount Zion to say farewell to those who were leaving. As the chosen ones filed out of the church at the end of the service the other children sang to them:

> Don't forget the Orphan Homes of Scotland,
> Don't forget the dear friends here;
> Don't forget that Jesus Christ your Saviour
> Goes with thee to Canada.
>
> And remember we are still a-praying
> That your life will be good and true,
> And that you may find a blessing
> In the land you're going to.

The next morning children and adults lined Faith Avenue to wave off the young emigrants; and when news of their safe arrival in Canada eventually reached the Superintendent, the bells of Mount Zion rang out around the village. The terrible sinking of the *Titanic* on April 14, 1912, when she hit an iceberg south of Newfoundland, caused a thrill of horror round the Homes—their party of boys had reached Halifax safely by the same route just a few days before.

Parties of children continued to leave for Quebec and Halifax throughout the 1920s, but the depression hit Canada very badly and she became unwilling to support immigrants from all over the world. In 1933 she closed her ports to them, and in the following year Fairknowe was sold. Altogether more than 7,000 had come west from Bridge of Weir since that first party of boys who gathered at the Broomielaw in 1872.

James McCallum is one of the 7,000. He was sent to Canada when he was 15 with a party of 40 boys, in April, 1929:

> I was asked if I wanted to go to Canada but I cannot remember by whom, and my answer 'yes' was just an impulse as up to that moment I had not dreamed of going anywhere, especially Canada.

There were no preparations for us prior to departure. No lectures, talks or anything that would prepare us for a new and strange life in Canada; but there was an interview with two officials of the Canadian Department of Immigration.

These interviews were conducted separately and privately for each boy, and we were asked questions of general knowledge.

The Orphan Homes owned two buses, one large and one small, and we were taken to the ship in the big bus. It was the custom for all boys and girls to line the road leading to the main gates and cheer us on our way. I can remember leaning out of the bus window trying to spot my sister in the crowd and screaming her name so that she would notice me. As we drove out of the gates I had a lump in my throat that had nothing to do with the Orphan Homes. It was for this little ten-year-old girl whom I suddenly realised I was leaving behind, possibly never to see again.

When I was sent out to my first farm I remember getting off the train at Lansdowne, Ontario, and waiting to be picked up. Mr. Bradley arrived in a spring wagon drawn by two horses and his first words to me were, "You're not very big, are you?"

In April in Canada, the frost is coming out of the ground and at that time there were no paved roads around that district, so everything was mud and the first thing I had to buy out of my wages was a pair of knee-high rubber boots.

I was to get ten dollars per month in the summer and five dollars in the winter months; however, up to that time I had never seen a cow milked and could not have been of much use to him in the beginning.

I was very well treated by this man and his wife (they were not long married) and one of my jobs on Monday morning was to turn the crank of the washing machine for Mrs. Bradley.

Learning how to harness horses, and the names of the various parts of the harness was confusing. The horses seemed like giants to me and a horse is very quick to spot a greenhorn and take advantage. However, I learned quickly and in May, under supervision of my boss, I was working the horses in the field, preparing for spring planting.

The first summer in Canada was a lonely experience for me. I don't think I spent five cents out of my wages, except for clothes. There was nowhere to go and no way for me to get there if there had been.

We arose about 4.30 a.m. and worked as long as it was daylight usually about 9 p.m. It was the custom for all farmers to work such hours. Any farmer who did not would have been thought to be lazy by his neighbours, and no farmer wanted such a stigma attached to him. Of course, they were attrocious hours for a young boy to work, but it was usual for the time and nobody thought there was anything wrong.

Hundreds and hundreds of boys and girls like James McCallum began their careers in Canada in this way on the farmlands of eastern

An ex-boy from Canada, aged 79, visits his old cottage. He well remembers William Quarrier and his daughter Mary and was thrilled to retrace paths he had so often trod as a young boy. *Reproduced from the 1975 Annual Report.*

Ontario. It was a hard, uncompromising life; the children worked long hours in all weathers, learnt quickly and grew up even faster. From the age of 14, when they received wages, boys worked from 4 a.m. or 5 a.m. in the summer until nightfall; in winter the hours were shorter, but it often meant working in freezing temperatures and wild conditions. Wages were low, and although board and lodging were included, the boys and girls were expected to buy their own clothes and other necessities. The children were cheap labour, but they were completely untrained and, especially during the Depression years, infinitely better off than so many people who had no job and not enough money even for bread.

The boys did everything from felling trees to milking cows; they worked in the fields and drove the horses in ploughing and culivating; during the harvest they spent long back-breaking hours binding the corn into stooks and hauling the sheaves to the barns to be threshed. Girls, too, and children of school age were expected to help around the farm; in addition to housework, cooking, cleaning and looking after the children, many girls worked in the fields and tended the animals. Joan Scott went to Canada in 1910 and was adopted by a family near Brockville. Her adoptive mother was a widow, which meant there was a tremendous amount of farm work for the women of the household to do. Joan milked the cows, cleaned the stables, pitched hay, helped with the ploughing and harrowing, scrubbed floors and looked after the house.

The whole family was involved in farm work from the oldest to the youngest. Ellen Buck was 12 when she arrived in Ontario in 1911 and she should have gone to school for nine months in the year; but often there was too much work around the farm to be done;

> I got very little time to go to school. I was soon able to go for the cows, and help to milk, to feed chickens, pigs and calves. The Pritchards had a big farm with a large garden; many a time I cried with cold hands and broken nails, picking up turnips, of which we had many loads. The cattle were fed turnips once a day and we had to put the turnips through a chopper.
>
> Mrs. Pritchard was good to me and taught me how to bake bread, churn and make butter. We would spend a day killing and cleaning chickens for market where we sold the fowls, and butter and the eggs.
>
> I was glad when my sister Jessie was moved closer to where I was. It was five miles away. I would visit her on Sunday and ran back the five miles to help milk the cows.

But though the work was hard, generally the children were well-fed, clothed and housed. Plenty of milk, butter and eggs and three solid meals a day seems to have been the normal fare for most of them. And it was the custom for everyone in the house to eat at the same table—the older children employed as farm hands were not expected to eat apart from the family. Thomas Alexander lived in the Orphan Homes until 1945 and went to Canada on his own after seeing a poster in a railway station in Ayr, advertising the "land of opportunity". One of the things which impressed him most when he got his first job on a farm was that the hired man had his meals with the employer, something he had not experienced very often when he worked on farms in Scotland.

Generally the girls and boys had their own room in the farmhouse. Sometimes a boy would share a room with his employer or the son of the house, or a girl might share with the daughter. The farmhouses tended to be two-storey brick buildings with outside sanitation, although conditions varied according to how isolated the farm was. Catharine Wardle arrived in Ontario in 1928 and got rather a shock when she reached her new farm some miles from Ottawa and discovered how basic the amenities were:

> When we arrived at the farm I was shown my bedroom upstairs. When we came down I asked Mrs. Leach where the lavatory was. She took me outside and told me it was just round the corner. I was rather shocked when I saw it. I'd never seen anything like that before. I expected to see a flush toilet. But this was country living. I remember writing to my mother and telling her how backward they were in Canada.
>
> There was a hand pump in the kitchen so we could wash the dishes, but had to heat the water on the wood stove and if one wanted a bath one just took some warm water upstairs to the bedroom and filled the basin and had sponge bath. A basin and jug were kept in the room.
>
> There was no electricity then and we used oil lamps.

Life for the Homes children was certainly without any frills or concessions to age and inexperience, but there are mercifully few accounts of ill-treatment or unhappiness. The Quarrier organisation was by no means perfect, however, and some children did endure cruelty and harsh treatment at the hands of their employers and guardians in the years before tougher controls were imposed. The children were very vulnerable and completely at the mercy of the families they were placed with. They were dependent upon the distribution homes to find them good families and to visit them regularly to make sure things were all right. If these things were not properly attended to the consequences for the child could be harsh. Mrs. Wallace Smith's mother and aunt went to Ontario in 1889; her aunt, Katie, ended up with a family who treated her very badly:

> My aunt Katie could not eat rice pudding with raisins, but she was told that she had to eat it. That night, she vomited in her bed. For this she was put in solitary confinement in the cold for three days, then brought out and severely whipped. This she knew was going to happen all the while she was in confinement.

A Home boy learning to handle a plough
(Reproduced by Courtesy of the PUBLIC ARCHIVES OF CANADA)

Rose Loughheed's mother and aunt were also sent to Canada last century. Her aunt, Grace, went to a farm in a little place called Greenfield, in Ontario. She was only 8, separated from her sister and without anyone to turn to:

> The farmer drank excessively and sometimes beat her. Her teeth were very bad and she was overweight. One day at school she became hysterical. She was removed from that farm and sent to another where she received medical and dental treatment and was kindly treated.

It was this kind of situation, arising from poor selection and inspection of homes, that the *Glasgow Herald* was concerned about as early as 1883. In an editorial in February of that year the newspaper strongly criticised the lack of information available to the British public about just what went on at the Canadian end of juvenile emigration:

> We want to know, for example, what is done for the very young children who are sent out—whether they receive the education which they would be compelled to receive in this country if they remained here; whether at the most tender years they are not hired out to struggling farmers; whether they are treated with ordinary fairness, not to speak of ordinary humanity? . . . . Our Government have allowed this irresponsible deportation of the unprotected to go on without in any way troubling themselves about it.

The 1897 Act did make improvements, and Fairknowe Home tried to be diligent in its choice and inspection of homes, but even so, with only one or at most two visits from their representatives in a year, there was always the chance that a child could be mistreated. Some children were fortunate in finding very good homes, and people who took them to their hearts. Harry Braebner, for instance, went to work for a family in Ontario in 1920 when he was 15. He worked on that same farm for three years, still keeps in touch with the people and writes of them that they were "my first real family". The father of Glenna Morris, who lives in Athens, Ontario, was not so lucky, however. He was placed on a farm twenty miles from Brockville in 1910 where he was bullied and mistreated. No one from Fairknowe ever visited him to make sure he was well and happy, and he was quite alone. And yet this same boy later went to another farm where he was treated like a member of the family and regularly visited by Government officials and Fairknowe representatives.

THREE BROTHERS IN CANADA.
The eldest, sent to Canada in 1892, forwarded money to take out his two brothers.

This photograph and caption appeared in the 1901 Narrative of Facts

In general, though, the children from Bridge of Weir seem to have been fortunate in their new homes. The hardships they experienced were not due to ill-treatment or cruelty, but the shock of a strange land and unfamiliar people, the heartbreak of being separated from brothers and sisters, and the ache of loneliness in a place where they had very little contact with the outside world. William Beresford has been in Canada for over 50 years; he came out from the Orphan Homes in 1920, leaving behind his young brother. After the first year he wrote to the Homes at Bridge of Weir, saying, "It's real lonesome out here", and asking if his brother could come over and join him. His brother, however, did not want to leave Scotland and although the boys kept in touch, they remained on opposite sides of the Atlantic. William's was the loneliness of a thousand other young boys and girls all over Ontario. Martha Robb married a boy from the Orphan Homes whom she had known since he arrived in Ontario in 1911 and went to work for friends of her family. Martha's first memory of him was of a child who was "so quiet and always seemed lost". He had left his only sister behind in Scotland and here he was in a strange country, working for strange people who expected him to be able to do farm work for which he had never been prepared.

Ellen Buck remembers vividly her first days in Canada when she arrived with her sister in 1911:

> Quarrier had a home in Brockville where we were taken after landing, where we spent a few days. Jessie and I left at the same time, but she left the train before I did which upset me very much.
>
> I was met at the station by Mr. Andrew Pritchard. We had quite a long drive to his farm at Dunrobin. Mrs. Pritchard and their sons were all at home. It was a frightening experience for a shy twelve-year-old; I couldn't understand why they should laugh at my Scottish tongue.

Catharine Wardle was a good deal older when she came to Canada; she had just turned 18, but she too had to cope with a sharp sense of loneliness and awkwardness at first.

> The first Sunday I was at the farm I went to church with Mrs. Leach and her son. Just behind us I heard two girls whispering; one was asking, "Who's she?" The other girl said, "She's just one of these Home girls." Mrs. Leach had a girl from Quarrier's before. I really felt hurt when I heard this and I heard it quite often—"Oh, she's one of those Home girls".

The children were supposed to attend school until 14, and for those who did it was a chance to meet people of their own age and make friends. Otherwise there was little opportunity to leave the farm. The biggest social gathering in these remote country districts would take place at the local post office or church. The older children who were earning had all their wages put into a savings account which they could not touch until they were 18, so they had no money to spend on entertainment and outings even if any had been available. Charles Cummings found the different customs and the smallness of the community very difficult to adjust to at first when he arrived in Canada in 1921:

> Being under age, I had to attend school until I reached 14, mandatory under Canadian law, but this seemed a waste of time. I found it bewildering to have to cope with the different customs of the land, the different money system as well as the very different school curriculum. So as soon as I could, I quit school, as it seemed the end of the education line for me.
>
> Life has changed a great deal in Ontario since my early years there. In those years no one travelled far from home, entertainment was almost non-existent—in

fact it was neighbourhood gossip over the party-line telephone and church on Sundays. Since we orphans were scattered throughout the province of Ontario it was not possible to have any contact with the other boys. So, except for my brothers, I don't know what has become of the others. I think that this was very unfortunate.

It was not all frighteningly bewildering, though. There were some funny moments, too, like the day when Catharine Wardle discovered just how little she knew about the flora of Canadian farms:

> One day in the Spring I saw this lovely yellow flower by the fence. I picked it and set it in a dish on the kitchen table. When Mrs. Leach came into the room and saw this beauty she asked me where I had got it. I said, "By the fence"., "Well," she said, "if you had left it there, it would have turned into a pumpkin". Was my face red!

The children from Bridge of Weir were survivors. They endured the loneliness, they worked hard and saved hard and made lives for themselves across the length and breadth of Canada. As Charles Cummings writes, "Few, if any, got rich and none became Prime Minister as was suggested we might when we left the Home in Scotland"; but they were all pioneers, made independent and determined by necessity. Thomas Duncan went to Canada with his sister, Elizabeth, at the age of 11, and his niece, Helen, writes with pride of the way brother and sister succeeded in building lives for themselves. They were placed with families near each other and Elizabeth continually supported Thomas in his schooling. She used her small wages to buy the books and clothes he needed for High School, and even gave him the money she had been saving up to buy a sewing machine for herself. Thomas managed to go to university, encouraged and helped through it all by his sister; eventually the young Scots boy who had come from an orphanage to work on a farm in Ontario ended up as the Professor Emeritus of Greek at Washington University in Missouri, U.S.A.

Today they are living all over Canada, these men and women who started life with so little, and ended with homes and families. James McCallum counts himself among those who have made a good life for themselves over there:

> Canada was fortunate indeed to receive such future citizens; it was Scotland's loss that they were sent away.

This dramatic sketch highlighting the unhealthy conditions in Glasgow houses appeared in the "Bee" magazine of October 7th, 1874

(Reproduced by Courtesy of THE MITCHELL LIBRARY)

CHAPTER SEVEN

The Pioneer

THE LAST FEW years of William Quarrier's life were spent as industriously and enthusiastically as ever. Far from being content to sit back and keep a paternal eye on the activities of the Orphan Homes and the City Home and Mission, Quarrier wanted to extend and diversify his work. While hundreds of his children made the journey across the Atlantic to far-off places, he too was exploring new horizons at home in Bridge of Weir.

It was typical of Quarrier that he should focus his attention on and direct his energies towards an area of contemporary concern. When he formed his Shoeblack Brigade and opened his first children's homes, Glasgow's pauper children were a scandal of the day. His many years' experience of the dreadful physical condition of the children he had helped now galvanised Quarrier into action against another scourge of the nineteenth century — tuberculosis.

Anyone who has ever read a Victorian novel will have come across the frail consumptive heroine, like Helen Burns in *Jane Eyre,* who grows weaker and thinner with coughing as each day passes. Quarrier encountered many young boys already debilitated by the disease in his Industrial Brigades, and each day he admitted children to his Homes who had lost one or both parents through its ravages.

For tuberculosis was a killer a hundred years ago in Britain. The disease took a terrible toll in nineteenth century Glasgow and the statistics make grim reading. In the period from 1855 to 1864 it was responsible for 13% of the total death rate in the city; in 1875, together with bronchitis, it accounted for 47% of all deaths. Tuberculosis was just one of the many diseases which spread easily in a city notorious for its overcrowding, bad housing and poor sanitation. From the early years of last century until the 1870s, Glasgow regularly fell victim to all kinds of epidemics; typhus raged in the city for a year in 1818 and broke out again in the 1820s and 1830s; 3,000 died within the first ten months of a cholera epidemic in 1832. And both diseases struck again and again throughout the city during the middle decades of the century.

People did gradually become aware of the importance of things like proper sanitation for preventing the occurrence and spread of disease, and by the second half of the century measures were being taken to ensure better public health. Fresh water was piped to the city from Loch Katrine in 1859, Glasgow appointed its first Medical Officer of Health, Dr. William Gairdner, in 1863 (a year after Edinburgh appointed their first one, Dr. Littlejohn) and fours years later the first Public Health (Scotland) Act was passed.

These and other measures, like better housing, contributed to the decrease in the number of deaths from tuberculosis after the 1870s; and after Robert Koch published his discovery of the bacillus of the disease in 1884, towns and cities took steps to control the sale of food and milk which might carry the infection. But although there was growing awareness of what caused tuberculosis, apart from ordinary infirmaries there were no facilities for its treatment in Scotland. Quarrier wanted to change this.

He first broached the subject as early as 1888 in his *Narrative of Facts;*

> For some years past, we have greatly felt the need of a house where older boys suffering from consumption and other diseases could be cared for. To build a Home for this purpose, £2,000 would be required, and we look to the Lord to incline one or more of His stewards to do this piece of service for Him. Bethesda, our Home for Invalid girls and little boys, has been fully occupied throughout the whole of the year, and as four of our older lads have died in the Infirmary—where we had to send them, not having a separate place to nurse them in—and many consumptive and delicate ones have had to be refused admission to the Homes, we are very desirous to have a house where we would be privileged to care for such.

At this stage Quarrier envisaged a new home especially for consumptive children where they could be isolated and treated away from the healthy ones. But by 1893, when he returned to the subject, he had a much bigger project in mind. In the *Narrative of Facts* for that year he proposed to build two hospitals on land adjoining the Orphan Homes, one for females and one for males, where anyone from the age of 4 to 30, who was orphaned or destitute, could be treated. The hospitals were to be for old and young, men and women, for the whole of Scotland— and they would be free.

Quarrier had done a good deal of research and had travelled round England visiting the Royal National Hospital for Consumption at Ventnor, on the Isle of Wight, and the Hospital for Consumption in London. The Brompton Hospital, opened in 1846, was built on the block and ward system of an ordinary infirmary and could accommodate nearly 350 patients, but Quarrier preferred the set-up at Ventnor; there the patients lived in separate rooms in spacious airy houses which reduced the risk of infection. This was what he had in mind for his own hospitals—there would be two separate blocks with accommodation for 20 patients, and each patient would have his or her own room, or at the most share with one other person. There was no such place in Scotland. As the 1893 *Narrative of Facts* said, this would be the country's first free consumptive hospital and Quarrier believed it would be a success.

Within weeks of announcing his plans for the hospitals, Quarrier had received the promise of £7,500 to build the first one, and other donations followed quickly. He had had his eye on the farm of Carsemeadow which adjoined the Orphan Homes, and when it came on the market he stepped in and bought 86½ acres for £6,722. Building could now begin and on September 5, 1894, the foundation stone of the first hospital was laid. It was a bold and responsible undertaking and Quarrier had surrounded himself with the leading medical men of his day as an advisory board, among them Dr. William Gairdner and Dr. James Russell, both former Medical Officers of Health for Glasgow.

After the excitement and expectation of the laying of the foundation stone, hopes of admitting the first patient within just two years were

The laying of the memorial stone of the Consumption Hospital by Sir William Arrol, September 5th 1894

high, but things did not go according to plan. Work began on the first hospital and the executive buildings, where the steam boilers, Turkish baths and inhalation rooms were to be housed and both were officially opened on September 3, 1896; but it was to be another two years before the first patient was admitted. Problems with drainage and the new sewerage system caused many headaches for Quarrier and he must have wondered if his hospital would ever be ready.

But at last it was. On May 27, 1898, the first woman patient was admitted to Scotland's first hospital for consumptives. This "Riviera in Renfrewshire", as it had been dubbed at the official opening, was ready to receive women from all over the country and try to effect a cure for their suffering. But it became evident after only nine months that the system of warm-air ventilation was not having the desired results—it seemed that the Riviera regime of steam baths, inhalation sessions and heated bedrooms did not improve the health of the patients significantly. So, after a year, and just a few months before a second hospital for women was opened, Quarrier announced a change of treatment and a change of name. Instead of pumping warm air into all the rooms to keep them at a constant high temperature, he adopted the Continental open-air system which meant plenty of fresh-air and outdoor exercise in all weathers for the patients. The ventilation machines were switched off, all the windows were thrown wide open, day and night, and the Consumption Hospitals at Bridge of Weir became the Consumption Sanatoria.

In the *Narrative of Facts* of 1899 Quarrier gives a vivid account of this new treatment which every patient underwent, or rather, I suspect, endured:

> The patients usually reach us with the temperature varying from 100 to 103, and on arrival they are sent to bed until the temperature gets normal, the windows and doors of bedrooms being kept open night and day. During their stay in bed they must eat large quantities of food and drink quantities of sweet milk. After the temperature has reached its normal state, as shown on the chart marked daily, the patient is allowed to rise and go out, the doctor regulating the length of walking exercise to be taken. The patients are not allowed to walk out in large numbers, but alone or with one companion, so as to avoid excitement in talking. The rising hour is seven o'clock, and after bathing, dressing, etc., breakfast is served at eight o'clock, consisting of ham and eggs, fish or other meats, with a good supply of

bread and plenty of butter, a pint of warm milk, and finishing with a cup of tea, if desired. After breakfast and examination by the doctor, they walk out in all weathers, returning to the house at 12 o'clock to rest for an hour before lunch at one o'clock. This meal consists of roast beef, mutton, tongue or other beef, amounting to half a pound after being cooked, to each patient, with potatoes and other vegetables and followed by a good supply of pudding. A pint of sweet milk is also taken with this meal. If patients cannot eat there is little hope of recovery, and it is necessary on their part to exercise a good deal of will power, as well as supervision on the part of the doctor and nurses, to see this part of the treatment carried through. The doctor presides at meals, and insists that, even if they have to sit for two hours or more, the quantities prescribed must be partaken of . . . The afternoon is mostly occupied with short walks and rest in the open-air couches, or, when stormy, in the open-air shelters provided in the grounds. Rain does the patients no harm, and they are out in all weathers. A mackintosh is not allowed to be used, as it causes perspiration . . . After an hour's rest, dinner is served at seven o'clock, where, as at lunch, half a pound of meat, with potatoes and vegetables, etc., must be disposed of by each patient, followed by a good supply of pudding, and finishing up with fruit and plenty of sweet milk. After dinner there is quiet rest, and all must be in bed by nine o'clock, with windows and doors open all night.

It's a fascinating account of the earliest methods used to tackle a killer disease without any of the tuberculin injections and chemotherapy which were developed years later. Apart from stuffing their patients with food and drink, all that the doctors at the Sanatoria could do in these early days was to try to guard against infection by burning the patient's handkerchiefs every day and regularly examining their sputum under the microscope until no trace of the tuberculosis bacilli could be detected.

Until 1901 the Sanatoria at Bridge of Weir remained the only place in Scotland for the special treatment of the disease. In that year the Glasgow and West of Scotland branch of the National Association for the Prevention of Consumption, formed at the turn of the century, donated £500 towards the cost of a Sanatorium at Bellefield in Glasgow; and three years later they recognised the pioneering work at Bridge of Weir by granting £5,000 to the Sanatoria over five years. A third Sanatorium, for men, was added to Bridge of Weir in 1907 which made it the largest centre for the treatment of consumption anywhere in Scotland.

The year after the Congress on Tuberculosis which Quarrier attended in London in 1900, Queen Victoria died. When she acceded to the throne in 1837 William Quarrier was just eight years old and starting an apprenticeship as a shoemaker; on her death she left behind a British Empire which ruled a quarter of the world's peoples and was more powerful and influential than it had ever been. Quarrier was 72 when Victoria died. In the thirty years since he opened his first home for orphans in Renfrew Lane, 13,000 children had passed through his hands and over £500,000 had been sent in from people all over the world. His Orphan Homes at Bridge of Weir had grown into a village with everything from a church to a fire station, inhabited by many hundreds of children. And he had given Scotland its first free sanatoria for consumption.

He launched his last big project in 1901, one which he had been thinking about for many years. In his 1893 *Narrative of Facts* he had described some of the terrible physical disabilities suffered by the orphans he had been dealing with for nearly thirty years;

> During the 29 years of our work amongst poor children we have had under our care about 10,000 children and young people. Among these there have been many deformed, helpless and incurable ones. Some of these have been born without hands, others without a leg; some of them being worsted in the battle of life, have lost some of their members, and again others have spinal and hip-joint diseases, while some are afflicted with epilepsy, a most distressing form of disease.

It was this last class of sufferers, people with epilepsy that Quarrier now wanted to help. Very little was known about the condition; it was known as "the falling sickness" and an ignorant and superstitious public believed it to be a form of insanity. In tackling the problem of epilepsy, Quarrier was stepping into even more unexplored territory than the treatment of consumption had been. There was nowhere in Scotland where someone with epilepsy could be helped, but in England new ideas about how to treat the condition had been developing over the last few years. Europe saw the first examples of small communities, usually in rural areas, where people with epilepsy could live and work, away from the prejudices and pressures of life in the outside world. The practice spread to England, and many such communities—or colonies, as they were named by the enthusiastic pioneers who started them—began to appear all over the country. In 1901 Quarrier visited one of the most well-known, the Chalfont Colony for Epileptics, in Buckinghamshire, opened in 1893, where 136 men and women lived in six houses, supervised by staff. The colonists lived and worked together with the staff, were taught trades and did light work each day. Quarrier also visited the Maghull Home for Epileptics, near Liverpool, which was run on similar lines.

Scotland was far behind England and the rest of the civilised world in treating epilepsy, and there were no such centres anywhere in the country. The poorhouse or asylum were the only places for men, women and children with epilepsy whose family could not look after them, or who had no family, and Quarrier estimated that there were some 4,000 sufferers all over the country. He wanted to build a Colony of Mercy for them, as he called it. His plan was to buy more land beside the Homes and build six houses, rather like the children's cottages, two for men, two for women and two for boys and girls, at a cost of about £20,000. There the colonists would live together in a home-like atmosphere, doing light work such as gardening, getting plenty of outdoor exercise and helping round the village. Like the Sanatoria, the Colony would be national and anyone from Scotland would be eligible for admission for a small weekly charge.

Donations began to pour in from all over the country, and in 1902 Quarrier bought 213 acres of Hattrick Farm which adjoined the Homes land. He had consulted closely with many medical men, but in these early days before powerful drugs and advanced electronic equipment for scanning the brain had been developed, the Colony of Mercy could only offer healthful air and pleasant, open surroundings which Quarrier hoped might relieve some of the anxieties and stresses of the patients. He described it in this way in the 1902 *Narrative of Facts:*

> Our aim is to provide this open door where afflicted ones may be sent with the assurance that all that medical skill and sanctified common sense can do for them will be lovingly rendered.

"Sanctified common sense" —what an apt description of the characteristic which informed all of Quarrier's work.

COLONY OF MERCY FOR EPILEPTICS.

WE give our friends above a more finished picture of the first house in the Colony than we were able to furnish in last report. It will be seen that the place is gradually taking on a more " homelike " appearance. This house was opened more than three months ago and is proving well suited for the object for which it was designed.

Reproduced from the 1906 Narrative of Facts

William Quarrier did not live to see the opening in 1906 of the first home of what was, and still is today, the only place in Scotland exclusively devoted to the treatment and care of people with epilepsy. A year after he had bought Hattrick Farm, and just two weeks short of completing thirty-nine years of work with Scotland's children, William Quarrier died, on October 16, 1903.

He had become ill at the beginning of the month with the kidney trouble which dogged him all his life. His condition became alternately better and worse until at midnight on Tuesday, October 13, he suffered a stroke which left him paralysed down the right side. He never properly regained consciousness and died in the early hours of the Friday morning. Thousands attended his funeral from far and wide and the flag above the City Chambers in Glasgow flew at half-mast. Friends and relatives, workers and colleagues, joined hundreds

The gravestones of the Quarrier family in Mount Zion churchyard

of children in the Homes Church, Mount Zion, for a simple service, and afterwards William Quarrier was buried in the little cemetery in the grounds of the church. The inscription on his coffin read:

> Entered into rest, October 16, 1903, aged 74, William Quarrier, friend of the poor and needy, and founder of the Orphan Homes of Scotland.

Quarrier's son-in-law and right-hand-man, David J. Finlay, described him as Scotland's greatest philanthropist; the obituary in the *Glasgow Herald* said that a unique personality had been lost. Quarrier **was** a compelling figure, a man years before his time who, single-handed, challenged grave social problems with which the public authorities of his day could not cope. He was spurred on always by an acute sense of personal responsibility, as a Christian and as a member of the community. He had suffered great privation and hardship himself as a boy; as he grew up, he saw the same need and distress all around him, and he knew that he must fight it.

He was a man of incredible energy and enthusiasm who was always seeing new work to be done, always interested in every aspect of the work in progress. There is a story that during the construction of the first cottages at Bridge of Weir he could often be seen out early in the morning, checking the walls with a spirit level. He loved to be in the thick of things and there was a strong streak of the fighter in him, that same streak which helped him survive a hard childhood and brought him success as a businessman.

Everything he did had flair and dare. He once challenged the editor of the *Glasgow Herald,* who had criticised his emigration work, to come with him into the heart of the city slums and see the kind of children he was trying to help: "See for yourself the misery and wretchedness which it is impossible to describe" he wrote to the editor, and "accompany me with a band of rescued ones to Canada". If the editor found Quarrier's claim that the majority of his children did well in new homes in Canada to be wrong, Quarrier would pay all his expenses for the trip; but if not, the *Glasgow Herald* would have to foot the bill. The editor did not take up the challenge.

Quarrier was a man who liked to get his own way and he was no diplomat when it came to getting things done. If something had to be done, he preferred to do it himself and would brook no interference once he had made up his mind that something was right. With committees of any kind he had very little patience, and although he worked with a great many dedicated helpers, he always liked to forge ahead on his own.

But with this strong and determined personality went great compassion and warmth. A Scot through and through, his outward manner, rather stiff and reserved, often belied an inward warmth. No one but his wife and family knew, for instance, that for more than twenty years after the death of Thomas Corbett, who gave the original £2,000 for the Renfrew Lane Home, Quarrier visited his grave every year and laid flowers there. Throughout all those years of building Homes and helping Scotland's children, William Quarrier never forgot the man whose kindness and generosity had made it all possible.

CHAPTER EIGHT

Cottage Life

. . . The car sped on through towns and villages; within a mile or two of our destination the scenery became very pleasant, with green fields and horses and cattle grazing peacefully; the sun was shining a little, too. Maybe it wouldn't be so bad in a home after all, I told myself at one point on the journey, but deep down inside me I was filled with a terror I had never known before in the short life already behind me. I tried to comfort my sister. There was someone else in the car carrying a very young baby, but she didn't take much notice of us, or I of her.

Isabel clung to me more than ever when she realised that we were approaching our destination.

We were now travelling on a very narrow road; the car had by now slowed down considerably. Soon it turned into a driveway. We had arrived.

Eventually two pathetically-clad waifs entered the hall of the big grey house that was to be my home for seven and a half years and Isabel's for over three years.

We waited in the hall for a few minutes. It was a large square hall with four doors leading into rooms. However, my very first observation was not the amount of doors but a picture which hung above the door which faced the front entrance to the house. It was not really a picture at all; there were no lakes or trees on it, just words. The words I read were surrounded by little flowers and read thus: 'Christ Is The Head of This House, the Unseen Guest at Every Meal, The Silent Listener to Every Conversation'. Many times from that day I read these words and thought about them and wondered.

The day Jan Gordon arrived for the first time at the Orphan Homes of Scotland with her young sister is still vivid in her memory. Jan was just eleven years old and when she arrived that day at Bridge of Weir she had no idea why she was there, why her mother couldn't look after her and what was going to happen to her. What would life be like in this unfamiliar place?

What *was* life like for the boys and girls in the Orphan Homes? What was it like to live in a cottage with 30 other children, and how did the cottage function from day to day? Jan entered the Homes in 1939, thirty-six years after the death of the founder. But she would have found cottage life little changed from the early years of the century, for by the time William Quarrier died he had set in motion a pattern of life in the community he had created that continued in much the same way for half a century.

There were of course changes in management after Quarrier's death. The running of the Homes was taken over by his wife, Isabella, with an advisory council that consisted of Pastor David Findlay (Quarrier's son-in-law), Robert Bryden (the Homes architect) and Glasgow Councillor J. P Maclay, a long-standing Trustee. A statement issued by the Trustees announced that everything would be run as before and no appeals would be made for funds, in accordance with the principles on which Quarrier had founded the Homes. Less than a year later, in June, 1904, Mrs. Quarrier died and was buried beside her husband in the cemetery of Mount Zion. Now the management of the Homes, with their 1,200 children and two Consumption Sanatoria, fell to Quarrier's daughters, Mary Quarrier and Mrs. Agnes (Quarrier) Burges. Their sister Isabella, who was married to Pastor Findlay, did not join the Council of Management until 1931 when Mary died. The task ahead of the Quarrier family and the Executive Committee (as the Advisory Council was re-named in 1906) was a daunting one; thousands of men, women and children in the Homes were dependent upon them. But they shouldered their responsibility and the work continued.

For the children in their cottages daily life was not much affected by the changes at the top. Numbers in the village remained fairly steady; there was an all-time peak during the First World War — on Armistice Day, November 11, 1918, 1,550 children were resident — but throughout the inter-war years numbers were always around the 1,000 mark.

The cottages remained more or less as they had been built and were not extensively altered and re-decorated until the 1950s and 1960s. The open-sided sheds attached to each cottage, where traditionally chores such as cleaning shoes and cutlery had been done by the children, were not closed-in until 1949. More cottages were added over the years for babies and toddlers, but, essentially, the system of cottage life which Quarrier had inaugurated continued in much the same way until after the Second World War.

Christmas was a symbol of this continuity. Not until 1942 did the Homes end the old Scottish tradition of celebrating Christmas at New Year instead of on December 25. The children had to wait until New Year's Day to meet Santa Claus and receive their presents; instead they celebrated Christmas morning with a special breakfast of bacon and eggs (instead of the usual porridge, bread and margarine). The children were always making up songs about their life in the Homes and one which many Old Boys and Girls remember was about that special Christmas Day breakfast;

> There is a happy land
> Down at Bridge of Weir,
> Where we get ham and eggs
> Once every year.
> Oh, how the children yell
> When they hear the breakfast bell,
> "Oh, crickey, what a smell!"
> Down at Bridge of Weir.

Usually the cottages were decorated with streamers and coloured paper, but there were no presents round the tree — there was not even a tree. Instead the children would get an apple, an orange and a bag of sweets or a bar of chocolate in their black woollen stocking, and would spend the day quietly in the cottage. The real festivities took place on New Year's Day. A special service was held in Mount Zion and on the great day each child received a present from one of the three huge Christmas trees — a tree for the boys, one for the girls and the other for the sick children in Bethesda and Elim Homes and the Elise Hospital. The gifts were always brand new — toys, games, books and dolls bought by the staff from a list of things the children wanted. It was always a time of great excitement when your cottage

Hoop House, near Dunoon

mother asked you what you wanted for Christmas. There was, alas, no guarantee that you got what you asked for, however — one Old Boy remembers his disgust at receiving a Bible after he had asked for a pair of leather gloves.

The Homes did their children proud on such special occasions. Even during the straitened circumstances of both World Wars, years when prices shot up, when sweets and sugar were rationed and soldiers got most of the chocolate that was going, the children at Bridge of Weir never missed their Christmas and New Year's treats. Donations from an ever-generous public continued to flood in throughout the particularly severe years of the First World War. Even in 1916 when the cottages were bursting at the seams with soldiers' children, and food costs had soared (the Homes butcher's bill rose from £4,000 a year to £6,000 in just two years), still the *Narrative of Facts* could report that every need had been met and the accounts balanced.

Two weeks holiday down the Clyde was another special time for the children. In 1919 a friend gifted two houses on the Firth of Clyde near Dunoon — 'Torr Aluinn' and 'Hoop House' — for the exclusive use of the Homes, and each summer large parties of children travelled down for a holiday. Many of the orphaned, abandoned, desperately poor and ill-treated children who came to the Homes would never normally have had a holiday, and for them this was a thrilling time. All the girls received new summer frocks and hundreds of pairs of sandals were issued for those long days on the beach.

The parties consisted of about 250 children. On the great day the older ones marched in an enormous two-by-two crocodile to Kilmacolm Station, 2½ miles away, the younger ones going on ahead by bus. The excitement would mount as everyone packed into the train for Gourock and then, what delight to arrive at the busy quay and board the steamer! John Howatson was in the Homes in the 1930s and still remembers vividly the fun of that trip down the Clyde:

> Hunter's Quay, Kirn, Dunoon, all the hustle and bustle of quayside activity; and, after leaving Dunoon there was the preparation of watching for the first glimpse of Torr Alluin which stood on a raised mound of ground with a central tower, and from the tower someone frantically waving a tablecloth; tremendous cheers emitted from many throats, many Paisley design hankies were held up to flutter like flags. Then the Skipper blew a long blast from the ship's whistle which drowned out our cheers.

Housemothers would give out sandwiches during the trip and word always got around if cottage 41 was on board. The mother of that cottage, Ma Broon as she was known, used to make her boys spiced dumpling for the voyage, and there was always plenty left to share out with others.

Each child was given pocket money to buy sweets or trinkets during the holiday. Catharine Hopkins, who went to the Homes in 1906, remembers that when she used to go on holiday to another Homes cottage in Rothesay the great favourites to buy with your holiday penny were treacle toffees, four Blackjacks (sweets), a rubber ball or a skipping rope. Then there were all the usual games on the beach — races, sandcastle competitions, throwing competitions, looking for shells and lots of inter-cottage games, and sometimes, when invention had been exhausted, the children sat in groups on the sand and sang songs; like the one about the infamous Buck Ruxton who murdered

Torr Aluinn, near Dunoon

his wife and who, the children would whisper, owned the blue boat
anchored in the bay below Torr Aluinn:

> Blood stains on the carpet,
> Blood stains on the knife,
> Oh. Doctor Buck Ruxton,
> You murdered your wife.
>
> Nurse Mary was watching,
> You thought she would tell,
> Oh, Doctor Buck Ruxton,
> You killed her as well.

Holidays, Christmas, Hallowe'en, Easter — these were the
highspots, the red-letter occasions of every child's calendar. They
earned these treats, though, because the rest of the time they worked
hard. By the 1960s every cottage in the Homes employed cleaners and
other full-time domestic staff for the general running of the cottage.
The children helped with beds and doing the dishes, but most of the
work was done for them. Things were very different fifty years ago.
"We ran the place" said William McCutcheon, who grew up in the

Homelea and Paisley Home

Homes during the War. Every child in the cottage, from school age upwards, participated in the cleaning, scrubbing, polishing, cooking and mending which was done every day. In the early years of the century the older children were up at 5 a.m. to scrub the outside steps and pathway to the cottage; a full day's cleaning of the house, from top to bottom, had to be done before school.

The rising hour got a little later as the years passed and by the 1930s it was between 6 a.m. and 6.30 a.m. But the virtues of tidiness, cleanliness, hard work and the conscientious carrying out of each household chore did not change. Jan Gordon remembers in astonishing detail her first experience of this domestic efficiency. When she arrived at her allotted cottage she and her sister were taken upstairs for a bath:

The girls ran the bath, about three inches of lukewarm water . . . We were placed in the bath together and duly scrubbed with red soap and a scrubber which seemed to be made of nails. Our hair was washed with the black Derbac soap and rinsed and washed again. Our hair was fine tooth-combed. The girls were kindly to us, and were doing their job in the conscientious manner expected of them . . . Finally we were dried and clad in white starchy nightgowns and green slippers about two sizes too big. We sat on a form until the girls had cleaned the bath and scrubbed the wooden draining board on the concrete floor with a big scrubbing brush; then, still on their knees, they washed and dried the surrounding floor. The girls then folded the canvas towels used on us, neatly, and placed them in a laundry basket. Nothing, I learned, was ever thrown; everything was folded neatly; even the smallest undergarment 'out for washing' was folded meticulously.

Each task had to be done properly or it had to be done again. Even the youngest children had to learn this. They often began by polishing the cutlery, starting with the spoons. This was in the days before tins of silver polish, so the children had to mix up whitening powder in water and then rub it on. The spoons were easiest because of the large surface area; it was when you had to clean the forks and make sure that no whitening was left in between the prongs that it became tiresome.

Boot-cleaning was another daily task. Each cottage had a huge boot rack in the hallway with dozens of pairs of shoes, black ones for summer, brown ones for Sundays and special occasions, and black lace-up boots for winter. In the days before Cherry Blossom, shoes were cleaned by mixing big slabs of boot black in water and

Girls at work in the Wash-House

meticulously rubbing it into the leather. It was quite common for a child of seven or eight to have ten pairs of boots to clean every day after school.

Boys had to do all the domestic chores that girls did, from cooking to cleaning. When a boy reached school-leaving age he usually did a year's full-time work as a kitchen boy in his cottage. After this he would probably spend a year with one of the tradesmen in the Homes learning the basics of a trade to prepare him for the day he left at 16. The same applied to the girls, except that they would spend a year or so in the Laundry or Patch Room or helping in the Elise Hospital or Baby Homes. Most of the girls leaving at 16 went into careers as domestic servants or nurses.

From the age of about ten, boys and girls were allocated certain jobs for a few months at a time round the cottage, designed to give them all-round experience of looking after a home. The Bedroom boy or girl made all the beds, cleaned the dormitories and swept and polished the wooden floors. It was the job of the Playroom girls and boys to help dress the younger children in the morning and get them ready for school, as well as to clean and polish the playroom daily. Bathroom duty involved bathing the little ones and cleaning the bathroom thoroughly. Some cottages even had a Potato girl or boy who had to peel a mound of potatoes for the large family every day.

The fact that Boys' cottages were run the same way as the Girls' with boys doing the cooking, cleaning, scrubbing and mending themselves, meant that the Orphan Homes produced a generation of men who were every bit as competent around the house as women. These men could cook, sew, knit, darn and make rag rugs; they could polish wooden floors and brass bed-knobs; and it was nothing to them to have to wash, dress and look after half-a-dozen toddlers and young boys.

A typical day for the Kitchen boy would test the culinary skills of most women. Under his cottage mother's supervision he was responsible for providing three meals a day for thirty or more children. His day began at 6.30 a.m. when he was up and about preparing porridge for the breakfast. He had left the oats to soak overnight and a huge pan of water simmering on the open range. If he had banked up the range properly the night before it would be at just a nice temperature and easy to stoke up for cooking. While another lad set the table and another cut and prepared slices of bread and margarine, the older boys in the cottage roused the young ones. All this time the Kitchen boy was keeping a watchful eye on the massive pan of porridge, trying to keep it hot without burning it, thick but not lumpy, in time for the serving of breakfast at about 7.45 a.m. After breakfast everyone helped with the dishes and once the kitchen was cleared and the boys had left for school, the Kitchen boy would have to start cleaning the black range and preparing the food for dinner at 12.30 p.m. This usually consisted of soup and a main course, or a main course and pudding; mince, stew, dumpling, bread puddings — these were the staple meals. Sunday dinners consisted of roast meat of some kind, but most of the preparation for that was done the night before so that as little work as possible was done on the Sabbath.

After tea at 5.30 p.m. and cottage evening worship, the Kitchen boy was free to go out and play. Football, cricket in the summer, and rounders — Bridge of Weir was a great place for sport and the children spent hours, especially in the long summer evenings, playing in the Park. Other evening activities included the Girl Guides, the Boys' Brigade, the Young Lad's Christian Association and on Saturdays the occasional film show in the church.

Sundays were strictly kept. Quarrier founded the Homes on strong Christian principles and from the start it was his avowed intention not just to rescue children from the poverty and misery of the streets and feed and clothe them, but to educate them in the Christian life as well. Every cottage mother and father had to hold Christian beliefs and inculcate them upon the children. So much so that Catharine Hopkins, who left the Homes in 1920 to go into domestic service, thought that she had landed in the house of the devil because her mistress did sewing and other small chores on a Sunday! It was drummed into the children that it was positively wicked to break the Sabbath in any way. A walk in the afternoon, in an orderly cottage group, was the only activity allowed on a Sunday.

As well as family worship every day in the cottages, there were services at 11 a.m. and 6 p.m. on a Sunday in Mount Zion. Each cottage had its allotted pew in the church, and every Sunday the rows would teem with children of all ages and sizes. There was no regular preacher to conduct the services; until the appointment of the then Chairman, Dr. James Kelly, as Honorary Pastor in the 1950s, services were conducted each week by visiting ministers from all over Scotland.

It was said by the children that Dr. Kelly always knew if a single child were missing from the Church services. And it was always a tense moment when he peered thoughtfully around the crowded hall, considering which cottage to ask to recite that week's text. This was a regular task set the children. The Homes issued a calendar with a different Bible text for each week. Every cottage was expected to learn the appropriate text by heart for the following week and be able to recite it faultlessly in front of the whole church if asked. Oh, the sinking feeling if your cottage was asked to stand up and recite and you hadn't learnt it properly! In earlier years it was the custom to choose just one child and there was an unspoken rivalry among housemothers to have the youngest child who could give a flawless performance. The younger the child, the more credit reflected on the cottage and the housemother. But if a text were wrongly recited, that was a black mark indeed and there would be trouble for the offender after the service. Anyone seen fidgeting, whispering or being inattentive was also liable for a telling-off or a clout back in the cottages. These services must have seemed endless to the younger children but at least they could join in the singing. Quarrier's children have always been, and still are, great singers. BBC Christmas broadcasts used to go out from the Homes Church and some years ago two long-playing records of the children singing were produced. "Sing with Quarrier's Children", on which the children sing some of their favourite hymns and choruses, was made in 1970 and eight years later a recording by the children of choral, solo and instrumental music was produced, called "Singing for My Lord".

Friday night was another special time of the week because that was when the cottage parents attended their own worship hour in Mount Zion. This was a time for fun and games since the children were left unattended. One Old Girl recalls the fun her cottage used to have sliding down the stairs on a mattress and playing the harmonium that was locked away in a cupboard in the playroom — someone discovered that the lock could be picked with the key from a corned beef tin! It was always considered very daring in the girls' cottages to pass messages to boys in school, inviting them round to the cottage on a Friday evening: not only was the mixing of cottages frowned upon, except in sport, but far worse than that was the mixing of boys and girls. It was not until 1945 that Dr. Kelly decided the time had come to experiment with mixed cottages for the youngest children.

Friday evenings offered opportunities for mischief and rule-breaking in an otherwise strictly controlled environment. Virtually every aspect of the children's life was regimented to some degree. Even brothers and sisters had to make an appointment to see each other outside school hours. The procedure was set down in the Homes' *Standing Orders*

> Brothers and sisters should be afforded reasonable opportunity of being frequently together, although not living under the same roof. In the case of brothers and sisters attending school, no special provision need be made, but where they have left school or are not yet old enough to attend school, boys should be given the opportunity on Saturday afternoons between 2 and 4 o'clock to visit their sisters. If they wish to do so boys should be permitted to visit their sisters on two Saturdays in the month. The limit of the visit should be one hour. Boys should be instructed to apply at the front door to the Mother of Home where the sisters reside. House Mothers of Girls' Homes will allow brothers to visit with their sisters in the Dining Room but not in the Playshed.

Of course the reasoning behind such rules was that with over 1,000 children in such a large place you could not afford to let everybody rush off and see their siblings whenever they felt like it, or it would end in chaos. In such a huge institution rules and regulations were necessary for the smooth running of things. But none of that was any comfort if it was *your* sister you wanted to see, *your* sister that you missed each day. James McCallum well remembers the chilling formality of his visits to his sister and how awkward and tongue-tied the unnaturalness of the situation made them both:

> I had a younger sister in the Orphans Home and in order to speak to her I had to make a formal appointment, and a day and hour would be named. I would walk up to her cottage and stand outside the fence around their play area. My

Dinner-time in Lincoln and Garfield Cottage

sister would come out and stand inside the fence, and because of the formality of the occasion I had no words except, "How are you, Georgina? Are you okay?" If they had allowed us to go for a walk together we would have had plenty to say to each other, but walking with a girl, even your sister, was strictly forbidden.

Everything was done at a set time and in a set way. When walking to church on a Sunday morning, many cottage mothers insisted that the children marched in a crocodile, two abreast, those on the right carrying their Bibles in their right hand, and those on the left flank carrying them in their left. In many cottages it was the practice for the children to march upstairs to bed at night, or march out of the house to school, in a long single line, the youngest first and the oldest bringing up the rear.

Mealtimes were nothing like the casual, informal affairs of today. No talking at the table was the rule in past years. Clare Macnair lived in the Homes from 1929 to 1943 and in her cottage not only did the girls have to file in to each meal in order of age, but had to show their clean white handkerchiefs to the Mother who stood at the door. There would certainly be trouble if you lost that precious cotton square; but if you pulled through a corner of your white apron so that it stuck up from your fist like a hankie, it was sometimes possible to escape retribution.

Generally, however, the children took the rules and regulations in their stride. For some, in the Homes since their earliest years, it was all they had known and it was a natural, accepted way of life. There was great camaraderie and friendship among the children in every cottage, a warmth and family feeling which was strong; the Homes were never a proper home but, as one former girl remarked, "The children made their own happiness", and for many, life at Bridge of Weir was far better than they would normally have had. "I never went hungry, I was never ragged," recalls David Wilson; "I never knew want, I never wanted for anything. In short, it was a better life and upbringing than I could ever have had with my mother".

But more than anything the quality of life in the Homes depended on the cottage parents, particularly the cottage mother. There were far too many children in each cottage for there to be much closeness and affection between mother and child, but there could be trust and kindliness. Most of the men and women who looked after the children were ordinary kindly people; they were not trained for the great responsibility and it can have been no easy task for a cottage mother fifty years ago who might have as many as 35 boys of all ages to look after all day. And in a place the size of the Homes it was inevitable that some cottage parents made a better job of it than others. Some former girls and boys remember their cottage parents with great affection; for them they were truly surrogate parents. Others were not so lucky and never enjoyed a close relationship. Martha Nixon came into the Homes in 1935 at the age of 8. Although her sister was in the same cottage, she desperately missed her real mother and could get no comfort from the cottage mother. "I never could cuddle or kiss her" she said, "She was terribly strict".

And there were an unfortunate few who have the awful and ineradicable memory of years spent with cottage parents who were not fit to look after children. Discipline for all children in the Homes was, by today's standards, strict; but there were a few men and women who most certainly punished the children in their care excessively, and in some cases treated them with unbelievable cruelty.

The memories of Jan Gordon, who was in the Homes from 1939 to 1946, read like something out of *Oliver Twist*. She has written about her life at Bridge of Weir in a personal narrative which she calls "Along Life's Narrow Way". The most harrowing descriptions in this vivid account are of the way in which her younger sister was treated. Her sister's crime was that she would not eat the lumps in her porridge:

> My sister was the worst offender. Miss Morrison★ . . . would drag her out of the seat by her hair, and make her stand beside the unlit fireplace facing the serving table; she would slap her about then push the plate into her hands. Sometimes she stuck her face into it, eventually castor oil was poured over it and she would be force-fed with the help of an older girl, Miss Morrison ramming it down her throat. . . If she was not at school she would be made to stand on her head in a corner of the hall.

Jan's sister was only five at the time. Such treatment would be almost impossible to believe if another girl who was in the same cottage for part of the time, from 1931 to 1941, had not duplicated some of the incidents recounted by Jan. Margaret Gatt describes the appalling treatment bed-wetters received in this cottage.

> In the morning you were punished by having castor oil poured over your porridge or tablespoons of Epsom Salts forced down your throat or sprinkled over your porridge; you willed yourself to keep it down . . . On the other hand you could be dragged up the stairs by the hair of your head, or by your feet, with your head bumping all the way up.

Bed-wetting seems to have been a common problem in the Homes. The *Standing Orders* refer to "the objectionable habits of children who are bed-wetters" and instruct House Mothers, in every case, to report it "to the Medical Officer and his instruction as to treatment carried out as far as possible. No treatment should be given apart from such direction". Despite these instructions, one "treatment" administered by callous housemothers in some cottages was for the child to be thrown into a bath of cold water. The earliest memory of Catharine Hopkins who went to the Homes in 1906 at the age of three, was being dragged downstairs by the hair and punished in this way because she had wet her bed.

★ *This is not the real name of that cottage mother*

Lessons over for the day at the Homes' School

The worst thing was that there was little help for it if a child happened to be in a 'bad' cottage. For children under the thumb of a cruel housemother or father, complaining was out of the question; they would probably be punished for that, too.Besides the children had virtually no contact with the higher authorities in the Homes and each cottage could function quite independently inside its four walls. In those days — unlike today when each child has their own social worker both inside and outside the Homes, and every cottage is regularly visited by all kinds of outside agencies — a child could be cruelly mistreated and few outside the cottage would know about it.

However, occasionally cases of extreme punishment did find their way to the ears of those in charge. This is a letter written in 1937 by the then chairman, Dr. James Kelly:

To the Fathers in Charge
   of the Boys' Cottages

I am sorry to have to write this letter but I do so at the request of the Executive Committee.

Several cases of extreme corporal punishment meted out to lads have been brought to our notice within recent date. One of these complaints has come from the Royal Scottish Society for the Prevention of Cruelty to Children, another from a donor and another from a Visitor. The receipt of such reports has vexed me very much. I do not wish to enter into the reason which may, or may not, have been the cause for the punishments, but I wish to express my own personal conviction with regard to excessive corporal punishment. Severe thrashing not only makes nervous wrecks of some boys, but hardens others, and produces defiance rather than penitence. It blunts the sensibility at a time when it is most desirable that the boy should be awakened by an intelligent understanding of his wrong-doing and an attempt made to secure a response to efforts for his welfare. A boy who has been severely thrashed loses respect for the person who did the thrashing. "Thrashing" is *wrong* and represents a denial of that which is of good in every boy, even the most troublesome.

I trust that all who receive this letter will accept it in the spirit in which it has been written and help to remove from the life of the Village this loathsome and, I believe, unnecessary form of punishment.

May I conclude by saying I am not unmindful of the difficulty of running either the Cottage or the Village life of our Community and I do appreciate the services rendered by all our fellow workers.

Last snapshot of William Quarrier, taken on the front at Millport, 11th August, 1903

It would be wrong and false to end an account of cottage life in the Homes in the first half of this century with stories of cruelty and beatings, for they do not represent the true spirit and quality of life for the great majority of children. Some, it is true, look back on their life in the Homes with great pain and bitterness, and with good reason. But they are outnumbered by those who remember Bridge of Weir with a positive sense of the chance for life which it gave them. At a time when many orphans went to the Poorhouse, and abandoned children did not have the protection of our present vast network of social care, the Homes at Bridge of Weir offered help and shelter. They clothed, fed, educated and brought up thousands and thousands of children who might otherwise have suffered great hardship.

Nellie Hood, who lived in the Homes from 1918 to 1927, is in no doubt of what she gained there:

> The Homes made me what I am today and I'm proud of what I am.

CHAPTER NINE

Changes

IT WAS MAY, 1941. On the sixth and seventh of that month the town of Greenock, William Quarrier's birthplace, was bombed by the Germans. And just a few miles to the south, across the hills, the children in the Orphan Homes of Scotland watched the glow in the night sky cast by the burning buildings, the whisky distillery and the sugar refineries.

The war years were exciting years for the children: hearing the bombers droning overhead on their way to targets all along the Lower Clyde; huddling together in the boxroom under the stairs until the 'All Clear', sipping cups of cocoa and nibbling bread and margarine; walking to school in the morning carrying your gasmask on your arm. Thrilling times for the children, perhaps, but air-raids and black-outs were a headache for the Superintendent and his staff. Blacking-out upwards of 90 buildings all over the village was a mammoth task and it was just as well that the policeman at Kilmacolm lived in a house overlooking the Homes — he could spot any chink of light from his vantage point and telephone the Superintendent to put it right.

The War did not disrupt the even flow of life very much at the Homes, but one or two sacrifices had to be made. The annual Hallowe'en procession with turnip lanterns had to be stopped because of the black-out, and the holiday homes at Dunoon — 'Torr Aluinn' and 'Hoop House' — were taken over by the Navy, and worst of all for the children, they had to watch while, one by one, the iron swings

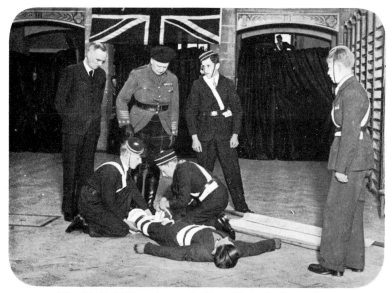

The Air Raid Casualty at the Boys' Brigade Inspection
From the Narrative of Facts for 1940

in the backyard of every cottage were dismantled and taken away to be melted down for the war effort.

But generally life continued much the same as usual. Rationing was not a problem and the Homes never went short of basic supplies since the farm at Hattrick was well-supplied with dairy cows and hens, and they had their own vegetable plots and greenhouses.

The war in Europe ended on May 7, 1945 — VE-Day. Eleven days later the news spread round the Orphan Homes village that Isabella Findlay, the eldest and last surviving daughter of the founder, had died. It was the end of an era. They were all gone now: William Quarrier and his wife, their youngest daughter, Mary, (who had died in 1931) and her sister, Agnes, who had died three years later. Pastor David Findlay, the husband of Isabella and, since Quarrier's death, an active force in the life of the Homes, had died in 1938. The only surviving figure from the early days was Lord Maclay who, as Glasgow Councillor John P. Maclay, had become one of the Advisory Council of the Homes on Quarrier's death. In 1926, when the Homes became a non profit-making limited company under the title the Orphan

Homes of Scotland, Lord Maclay acted as Chairman of the Council of Management. Now that post was held by Dr. James Kelly, but Lord Maclay was still closely associated with the Homes as Honorary President.

The end of the war marked 67 years since the opening of the Homes at Bridge of Weir. There were 1,227 children in the 43 cottages, referred from all over Scotland by officers of the R.S.S.P.C.C., by local authorities and directly by relatives. Over 200 of these children were babies and toddlers living in three cottages which had been built for them over the previous 15 years — Campbell-Snowdon, Laing-Shrewsbury and Campbell-Maltman Homes. The war had put a strain on the accommodation resources of the Homes; hundreds of children had lost a father temporarily or permanently; some had been made homeless by the bombing; others were admitted because their mother, with perhaps four or five other children to look after at home, simply could not cope. It all added up to lots of extra children and some cottages bursting at the seams.

Local authorities, too, faced the problem of children affected by

Ploughing for Victory *From the Narrative of Facts for 1941*

The Land Army *From the Narrative of Facts for 1942*

the War. Many boys and girls were evacuated from the big cities to safer areas and the local authorities had the responsibility of boarding them out. It was during this period of upheaval that concern grew about the plight of homeless children in public care. In England the case of Denis O'Neill brought to light the need for administrative reform in local authority machinery for the care of children. Denis and his two younger brothers and a sister had been taken from their home in 1939 by officers of the N.S.P.C.C. and handed over to the local authority, which boarded them out. In 1944 Denis was moved from one foster home and sent to another, a farm in Shropshire. Some months later, as a result of continual ill-treatment and neglect on that farm which the authorities were never aware of because no one checked up on him, Denis died. An independent inquiry under Sir Walter Monkton, K.C., investigated the whole incident and reported that there had been grave administrative muddles, a lack of effective supervision by the local authority social workers and, for that matter, a great lack of properly trained and skilled social workers.

Public attention had been drawn to the same question of children in care just a few months earlier by a letter which appeared in *The Times* on July 15, 1944. It was headed "Whose Children? Wards of State or Charity?", and was written by Lady Marjory Allen of Hurtwood, the wife of the First Baron Allen of Hurtwood, and the

Chairman of the Nursery Schools Association of Great Britain. Her letter was an eloquent expression of a new crusading spirit for reform which was emerging from the upheaval of war:

Sir,

Thoughtful consideration is being given to many fundamental problems, but in reconstruction plans one section of the community has, so far, been entirely forgotten.

I write of those children who, because of their family misfortune, find themselves under the guardianship of a Government Department or one of the many charitable organisations. The public are, for the most part, unaware that many thousands of these children are being brought up under repressive conditions that are generations out of date and are unworthy of our traditional care for children. Many who are orphaned, destitute or neglected, still live under the chilly stigma of 'charity'; too often they form groups isolated from the main stream of life and education, and few of them know the comfort and security of individual affection. A letter does not allow space for detailed evidence.

In many 'Homes', both charitable and public, the willing staff are, for the most part, overworked, underpaid and untrained; indeed, there is no recognised system of training. Inspection for which the Ministry of Health, the Home Office, or the Board of Education may be nominally responsible is totally inadequate, and few standards are established or expected. Because no one Government Department is fully responsible, the problem is the more difficult to tackle.

A public inquiry, with full Government support, is urgently needed to explore this largely uncivilised territory. Its mandate should be to ascertain whether the public and charitable organisations are, in fact, enabling these children to lead full and happy lives, and to make recommendations how the community can compensate them for the family life they have lost. In particular the inquiry should investigate what arrangements can be made (by regional reception centres or in other ways) for the careful consideration of the individual children before they are finally placed with foster-parents or otherwise provided for; how the use of large residential homes can be avoided; how staff can be appropriately trained and ensured adequate salaries and suitable conditions of work, and how central administrative responsibility can best be secured so that standards can be set and can be maintained by adequate inspection.

The social upheaval caused by the war has not only increased this army of unhappy children, but presents the opportunity for transforming their conditions. The Education Bill and the White Paper on the Health Services have alike ignored the problem and the opportunity.

Yours sincerely,

MARJORY ALLEN OF HURTWOOD

Hurtwood House, Albury, Guildford   July 15th, 1944

Less than a year after this challenging letter was written, and following on the Monkton Inquiry, two committees, one for Scotland and the other for England and Wales, were charged by the Government of the day to:

> enquire into existing methods of providing for children who, from loss of parents or from any other cause whatever, are deprived of a normal life with their own parents or relatives; and to consider what further measures should be taken to ensure that these children are brought up under conditions best calculated to compensate them for the lack of parental care.

The two committees, the Scottish one chaired by Mr. J. L. Clyde, K.C., and the English one by Miss Myra Curtis, spent 17 months investigating all aspects of the current care of children, both statutory and voluntary, and the recommendations they made were very similar.

The Clyde Report is a fascinating document, a compelling piece of social history which asks questions about the responsibility of the individual and society towards its children with the same earnestness that Quarrier had done in the previous century. The Report placed the emphasis, as Quarrier had, on recreating the family:

> The lesson which above all else the war years have taught us is the value of home. It is upon the family that our position as a nation is built, and it is to the family that in trouble and disaster each child naturally turns. It is the growing awareness of the importance of the family which has largely brought into prominence the problem of the homeless child. How then is the family to be re-created for the child who is rendered homeless?

There were, at that time, three ways of dealing with homeless children in Scotland: they could be boarded out with foster parents (a practice with a long tradition in Scotland); they could be sent to voluntary homes, like the Orphan Homes; or they could go into Homes provided by the local authorities (though these were far outnumbered by Voluntary Homes). Of these three solutions the Clyde Committee (and the Curtis Committee in England and Wales) strongly favoured boarding-out or fostering as the best and most natural way to create a good stable home for the child deprived of his real family. They were very much opposed to the 'outworn solution' of large institutions, the traditional orphanage of many hundreds of children in huge impersonal buildings. The Committee was more impressed by the Cottage Home system, but they stressed that if the numbers were not drastically reduced to no more than 15 children per cottage (at this time each cottage in the Orphan Homes housed more that 20) then the children could suffer just as much as in any large institution.

But the committee did not approve of fostering without reservation. As the Denis O'Neill tragedy had shown in England, fostering could go drastically wrong and the whole system needed to be be improved and reformed. There should be much more careful selection of foster parents, children should not be abandoned to the back of beyond in some remote Scottish croft (this was very common at the time), and supervision and visiting of the children should be tightened up. Even so, the report still saw the need for local authority and Voluntary Homes to provide for children not suitable for fostering, or who were coming into care for a short time only.

But the biggest stumbling block to achieving an effective, new, professional service for homeless children was the cumbersome and confusing administrative machinery which had been evolving for the past half-century. Statutory responsibility for the care of homeless children rested with not one, but three entirely different and separate bodies — Public Assistance Authorities, Education Authorities and the Department of Health. And in each case the children formed only a part of their areas of responsibility. "All this differentiation must go" declared the Clyde Report. It wanted to see a specially created body whose *sole* responsibility was the welfare of children and which would take over all the disparate functions of the existing agencies.

The 1948 Children Act made this proposed new committee a reality. Every local authority in the country was to set up a Children's Committee, headed by a Children's Officer, a trained man or woman appointed by the local authority and approved by the Secretary of State, who would oversee and organise a team of social workers to deal with the children in the Committee's local area. The Home Office was to be the sole responsible body at government level and would be advised by two Advisory Councils in Child Care, one for Scotland and one for England and Wales.

This enthusiastic and reforming Act was called "The Children's

Charter." At last homless and destitute children had been made a special case. Local authorities now had a duty to receive *every* homeless, abandoned or parentless child, not just those committed to them by the Courts under the Children and Young Persons Act of 1937. Very importantly, they were also required to restore a child to its parents or guardians, if it had any, as soon as possible; the idea now was to get children out of institutional care and back to normal family life in the community — an idea which would become the guiding principle behind all future developments in the care of children.

Training was also a priority in the Act. The Curtis Committee in England and Wales had been so appalled by the lack of trained staff, especially in residential homes, that it brought out an interim report pleading the need for a Central Training Council in Child Care which would initiate courses in subjects like child development, social conditions and the social services for staff in children's homes, and would encourage courses in child care at universities and colleges. The Children Act duly made provision for government grants to finance such courses.

A new child-care service had been created, the trained child-care worker was born, old ideas were passing and new ones emerging. And where did the Orphan Homes of Scotland stand in the midst of all this? They were directly affected by the Act under a clause which required every voluntary home to be registered and regularly inspected by local authority and government officials. Indirectly the Homes were to be affected very much more because the Act shifted the direction of child care away from residential homes to fostering, and charged state and local authorities seriously to address themselves to the task that charities and voluntary organisations had been carrying out for years. With fostering as the favoured form of care, and the onus on local authorities to try to return children to their real families, it was clear that the numbers coming into residential homes would eventually be affected. This was evident in the years after the Act came into effect: the number of children in the Orphan Homes after 1918 had remained fairly stable, at about the 1,100 or 1,200 mark, increasing sharply during the Second World War — but after the 1948

Act they decreased slowly and steadily, while the numbers fostered and in local authority homes increased.

But the Orphan Homes and the dozens of other voluntary homes still had an indispensable role to play in the care of homeless children, as the Clyde Committee concluded and the 1948 Act agreed. Accordingly, the Orphan Homes set about retrimming their sails for the task ahead. They set up their own training programmes for their staff and appointed a consultant psychiatrist to deal with the emotional and psychological problems which it was now recognised many children in care suffered from; they embarked on a modernisation programme for the cottages and began to reduce the numbers in each. And life inside the cottage began to change for the better; the atmosphere became less authoritarian and the children were allowed a little freedom. David Wilson, who was in the Homes from 1946 to 1956, remembers a gradual change in the 1950s

> Things did relax somewhat, with various excursions into the outside world, like visits to Port Glasgow Baths, the Baptist Chapel in Johnstone, visits to the Kelvin Hall Circus and Calderpark Zoo. There was also a visit to Edinburgh Castle and once I went to Hampden Park.

Television came into the cottages during the 1950s, and David remembers the thrill of watching TV for the first time, on the day of the Coronation of Queen Elizabeth on June 2, 1953:

> We sat glued to the set from dawn and never moved till transmission ended, drinking milk shakes and lots of goodies. We also received a Bible and a tin of toffees — a real special day.

Milk shakes and a Bible? Changed times, indeed.

1948 brought other changes to the Orphan Homes, this time as a result of the National Health Service Act. On July 5, 1948, the Consumption Sanatoria became the responsibility of the Western Regional Hospitals Board under the 1946 Act which brought hospitals under the administration of the Government through regional boards. The three sanatoria at Bridge of Weir had treated over 11,000 patients in the 50 years since the first unit was opened — 50 years that had seen the fight against tuberculosis won through increasingly

T.V.   I₂

The Coronation Parade

sophisticated methods of treatment and constant research. The sanatoria started by William Quarrier had led the way in Scotland and given vital care to thousands who would otherwise have died. Tuberculosis has now long been conquered in the western world, and the sanatoria complex at Bridge of Weir is now a geriatric hospital.

Before the 1950s were over, it was all-change once again at the Orphan Homes. Dr. James Kelly, Chairman of the Council of Management since 1937, had felt for some time that a new post should be created in management, a full-time position for a man who would devote all his energies to running the organisation in changing times. So, in 1956, Dr. Kelly was replaced as Chairman by Mr. William Marr (who had recently joined the Council) and the new post of General Director was created and filled by Dr. Romanes Davidson who had been the Medical Superintendent of the Homes and Colony of Mercy since 1946. The General Director would have complete control and responsibility for the whole organisation and would be subject only to the Council. It was a post which offered great scope for imaginative, bold leadership for the future.

And to the outside world, too, the Orphan Homes presented a changed look. The Homes had been started originally to give a home to Scotland's orphans — thousands and thousands of them; and at the turn of the century orphans still formed 85% of the children in the cottages. But this had been changing for many years, and by the 1930s the figure was considerably lower; the eradication of most of the dreadful killer diseases, like smallpox and typhus, had greatly increased life expectancy and children did not suffer the loss of both parents at one fell swoop as in the dark days of Victorian Scotland. It was not orphans now who formed the bulk of children in the Homes; instead there were children abandoned or deserted by their parents; the babies of unmarried mothers; children whose parents could not look after them because of illness or impossible conditions at home. In 1958, therefore, the Council of Management decided that the Homes needed a new name to reflect a new age and to honour the man who started it all. And so the Orphan Homes of Scotland became Quarrier's Homes.

It had been an eventful decade. Now, with a new name, a new man at the top and facing the challenge of adapting to new methods of child-care in changed times, Quarrier's Homes was set on a new course for the future.

CHAPTER TEN

After the Orphans

He needs to like children. He must have sympathy with, rather than pity for, their problems and those of their parents. He must understand their views of the world around them. If he is to help them to come to terms with society, he must not only know a good deal about that society and its standards and values; he must himself have come to terms with it and participate in it.

This is how a 1963 report on the *Staffing of Local Authority Children's Departments* described the qualities and abilities which every child-care worker should possess. Caring for children had become a serious professional business; the youthful, eager service which the 1948 Children Act had created thought about itself continually and kept a faithful note of all its doings, its new ideas and trial methods, and presented them to the world in copious reports, studies, memoranda and official documents throughout the 1950s and 1960s. A memorandum by the Home Office on *The Conduct of Children's Homes* in 1952 gave instructions on everything from the kind of staff who should be employed to the decoration and furnishing of the children's dormitories. The Scottish Advisory Council on Child Care (established by the 1948 Act) brought out numerous reports on children's homes and how they could be improved, on how children deprived of their normal home could best be cared for, on how important it was to understand the needs of every child in care and give him security and affection. Another regular contributor to Her Majesty's Stationery Office bookshelves was a series of reports on

Child Care in the 1960s, which kept up-to-date with all the latest developments in the field, produced statistics on the number of children in Homes and with foster parents, and kept note of the reasons for children coming into care, the numbers of child-care workers and the training they were receiving.

The training of staff was a common theme of this rapidly growing body of literature. The personal qualities of the Children's Officer and his fellow-workers — an ability to communicate, a sympathetic but professional approach — were highly rated; these were skills which could not be taught, but other skills, such as a knowledge of the other branches of social work which might bear upon the welfare of children, familiarity with the law relating to children, administrative skills — all these were vital matters for the child-care worker to learn. The problem was the lack of courses available in Scotland. There was huge need for trained men and women in the Children's Department but, according to the *Staffing of Local Authority Children's Departments,* not enough facilities for their training. The Scottish Education Department ran refresher courses for field staff (those who helped children in their homes and did not work in residential Homes), and for residential staff, and Langside College in Glasgow provided a course for Houseparents. Edinburgh University became the first university in Scotland to offer a certificate in child care.

Soon, however, these courses were buttressed by a multitude of others. A Training Committee of the Scottish Advisory Council on Child Care was set up to advise the Secretary of State on new courses, and by 1966 the situation had improved considerably. In addition to the university course at Edinburgh there was one at St. Andrews and a two-year course in child care at Moray House College of Education in Edinburgh; and plans were afoot for a one-year course for child-care officers with experience but no qualifications at Jordanhill College of Education in Glasgow. On top of that there was a host of short, non-certificate refresher courses for what seemed to be every subject under the sun, if the list in the 1966 report on *Child Care* is anything to go by:

> a general course for residential staff; a course for child care officers; a course for
> the staff of remand, reception and short-stay homes; a course for recent entrants

to child care field posts; a course for the heads of residential establishments receiving students for practical placements from residential courses; a course for staff who had recently started residential work with children; a course for child care officers, probation officers and other social workers working in isolation in rural areas; a course for the staff of homes and nurseries caring for young children; a course for staff concerned with adolescents in residential care; a course for child care officers and probation officers receiving students for casework placements; and a course for children's officers.

A great deal of the energies of Scotland's Children's Departments was devoted to fostering, and there was an urgent need for child care officers to deal with the organisation, placement and visiting of the huge army of children boarded out all over the country. The 1948 Act had given the official seal of approval to fostering as the most dersirable alternative for the child and by 1965, of the 10,457 boys and girls in the care of local authorities in Scotland, 60% were boarded out with foster parents, while 1,749 were in local authority homes and 1,646 in voluntary homes.

But although often the most homely and natural form of care for the child, fostering was still, like residential care, only a way of helping after the event, after the situation in the real home had broken down. What the children's departments wanted most of all was to prevent the child from having to come into public care at all; they wanted to keep the child with his parents wherever possible. So preventative work, as it was called, became another clarion call of the child care service in the 1960s. But what could child care officers do in the child's real home? The 1963 Children's and Young Person's Act made it a duty of the local authorities to give any advice, guidance or assistance to families which might help to prevent problems; for example children often came into care because their parents had been evicted for non-payment of rent, and child care officers could offer help and advise with budgeting to avoid this. The Act also empowered them to give actual financial aid if that was necessary.

This kind of preventative work and care of the child in his natural home continued to grow in the 1960s; and from there it was only a short step to the thinking behind the 1968 Social Work (Scotland) Act which abolished the children's departments and created in their stead new social work departments, administering all kinds of social services, including child care. The idea was to set up a wide-ranging *family service* which would be able to tackle all the kinds of problems that were very often behind the final event of family break-up and a child coming into care.

Against this rapidly moving background of child care, the numbers of children in Quarrier's Homes remained very much lower than in the years before the 1950s, but at a fairly steady level. The number kept around the 500 mark throughout the 1960s and into the early 1970s. Of the 43 cottages, about 30 were used for the children (the others had been converted into staff houses and used for other purposes, like extra accommodation for the Epilepsy Centre), with between 14 and 20 children in each. Things were very different in the cottages now. The days of scrubbing the bath with Bathbrick and cooking for 30 were long gone. There were still chores to be done, beds to be made each morning, shoes cleaned and washing-up after meals. At the weekend, too, there was some cleaning and dusting to be done around the cottage, but cleaners came in during the week and did most of the housework. Mealtimes were informal affairs now, eaten in the kitchen, at three or four separate tables. There was always plenty going on in the evenings and the long summer evenings often rang with the voices of hundreds of children playing in the park down by the school. On the Annual Sports Day, at Fancy Dress Parades and at Hallowe'en, the village thronged and milled with children of all ages and sizes. In the evenings they went to youth clubs, sports clubs and the uniformed organisations, and during the week went swimming, played hockey and football matches against schools from outside, and went to concerts and exhibitions.

Although the number of children living in the village was much smaller than in previous years, the turnover was higher. Children were coming into and going from Quarrier's Homes faster than ever before. They were there for shorter periods; years before when a child came into the Homes, it was usually for good, until school leaving age, but now many children whose home situation for some reason was not suitable were staying for perhaps just a few months or a year, until things at home had improved.

Another change from earlier years was the extent of local authority responsibility for the children. By this time most of the children were referred by local authorities and only rarely directly by relatives and friends. The local authorities were also funding each child they sent, so that, slowly but surely, the balance of the Homes income shifted away from donations and legacies from the public towards maintenance grants from the various local authorities. In 1960 local authority grants totalled £40,755 and donations and legacies, £181,202; by 1970 the figures were £171,161 and £216,912; by the late 1970s about 75% of the Homes' income was from local authority grants for the children.

These were fat years for Quarrier's Homes; donations and legacies from an ever-generous and solicitous public, supplemented by grants, kept the balance sheets very healthy, and enabled the Homes management to embark on a programme of renovation, repair and building around the village. It certainly needed a facelift; many of the buildings had not been touched since they were built nearly a century before. The Central Building, for example, was one of the very first buildings completed in 1878. In 1960 work began on its complete restoration and redecoration, and it was re-opened two years later as the new Somerville-Weir Hall, to seat 500. The cottages were thoroughly modernised and repaired — work which had been going on, too, during the late 1950s. The dormitories were made more homely and comfortable with carpets on the floors, bright bedspreads, little personal bedside tables and lockers, and the children's own pictures and posters on the walls. Downstairs the kitchens gradually acquired more mod-cons, with modern cookers replacing the old black open ranges.

The children got their own swimming pool, opened in 1966 by the Scottish Olympic champion swimmer, Bobby Macgregor. A brand new recreation centre was built two years later. On the site of the old training ship for boys, the *James Arthur,* a tuck shop was built where the children could spend their pocket money and lay in supplies of sweets for the week.

Outside the Quarrier's Homes complex there were other changes. The City Home at James Morrison Street which Quarrier had opened in 1876, and which for many years had been a home for working boys

Having fun in the Homes' swimming pool

in the city, had been sold in 1937. But this was not the end of the Working Boys' Hostel; the boys, about 20 of them, were moved to new premises at 1 Dumbreck Road, on Glasgow's south side, and a new hostel was established there in a house called 'Overbridge.' In 1965 it was converted into a children's home and in 1971 a final move was made to St. Andrew's Drive, Pollokshields, where 'Overbridge' is today.

Quarrier's Homes also kept up the long association with the Firth of Clyde coast which began last century when parties of children were sent to various houses in Dunoon and the surrounding area for their summer holidays. During the 1960s children spent the summer weeks in a holiday house in Girvan, a seaside resort south of Ayr. Not far from Girvan, on the estates of the wealthy industrialist, Mr. Niall Hodge, the Homes also had the use of several holiday cottages. Until his death in July, 1981, Mr. Hodge kept very close links with the Homes and gave generously of his time and money to make the cottages at Turnberry a marvellous resort for the children.

But the changes which really affected the fabric of life in Quarrier's Homes for the children and staff in this period took place within the cottages. The arrival of a new Superintendent started the ball rolling. After 24 years as Superintendent of the children at Bridge of Weir, Mr. Hector Munro retired in 1963 and his place was taken by Mr. Roy Holman from London. One of the first things Mr. Holman did on his arrival was to start mixing boys and girls in the cottages. This had been begun rather tentatively with the toddlers after the War, but even in the 1960s the majority of children still lived in segregated cottages, often separated from their brothers and sisters.

In 1965 Roy Holman returned to London and an Aberdonian, Mr. Joseph Mortimer, the present Deputy Director, joined Quarrier's as Superintendent and Deputy General Director, bringing with him highly professional credentials — he was one of the first male holders of the Certificate of Social Studies from Edinburgh University. He consolidated much of the work done by Roy Holman and introduced many more changes, improvements and new approaches to the work of the Homes, keeping Quarrier's moving with, and often ahead of, the times.

One of his main areas of concern was the training of staff. Traditionally, residential child-care workers had always lagged behind field workers in professional training. Residential work with children had been considered as something which could hardly be learned; the only 'qualifications' needed, it was thought, were things like common sense and the ability to understand children and run a house. Many men and women who had spent perhaps twenty years in the job were unimpressed by the argument that a more formal training would help them in any way with their job. But Mr. Mortimer felt that Quarrier's houseparents should be able to hold their own in the fast-changing, professional world of child care, with its increasing demands upon those to whom other people's children had been entrusted. He began to second some of his staff to child-care and social studies courses all over the country, and with his assistant, Mr. William Dunbar, devised new In-Service Training courses to replace those which had been going on in a desultory way since the 1950s. One day a week cottage parents from the Homes and other people from outside the village with a specific interest in child care matters, attended lectures and seminars on such subjects as child development, the problem of adolescence, the health of children and the importance of leisure time and how best to use it for the benefit of the children.

It was also during this period that the foundations of the present social work unit within the Homes were laid. The social workers provided much needed support and back-up for cottage mothers and fathers. It was gradually being recognised that looking after 15 or 20 children under one roof was a mammoth task for anyone and that more staff were needed in every cottage. Today each cottage has either a cottage mother and father, plus four assistant houseparents, or a cottage mother with five assistant houseparents, all working on a rota basis. There is also a cottage manager in charge of the smooth general running of a group of cottages. This situation certainly eases the strain on the staff, but on the other hand can cause problems for the child who has to cope with being looked after by so many different people.

Children in the Homes from the 1960s onwards enjoyed a very different lifestyle from their predecessors. They had more freedom to come and go, to visit Bridge of Weir and Glasgow at weekends, to go on group outings and mix freely with children from other cottages. However, it was still a sheltered environment, especially for those children spending years there from a young age. Far away from the city, this strange village of children was beautifully situated, free from pollution and heavy traffic, with wide tree-lined avenues and pleasant views. It was all so pleasantly rural that Elizabeth McLean, who spent several years at Quarrier's in the 1960s, got quite a shock when she returned to the city:

> The one problem I had when I left was getting used to traffic on the roads. When we were in Quarrier's there were no cars or very few that went through the Village, and to come and stay in a busy town was quite frightening for the first few weeks.

Increasing access to the outside world minimised the problems of isolation but there was also the problem of educating the children in the use of money. At that time everything necessary simply fell at their feet rather like manna from Heaven. The Store within the Homes had everything for the cottage, and cottage mothers simply filled in a form for what they wanted, handed it in at the counter and walked away with the provisions. The Drapery provided for all the clothing

The Boys' and Girls' Council with Mr. Mortimer

needs of the children and issued them with skirts, blouses, trousers and other articles whenever they were needed. The brown three-wheeled bread van came around the cottages every morning, and milk from the nearby dairy was delivered to each doorstep. Mr. Mortimer felt that it would benefit the children to be educated a little in the realities of money and what it could buy, so he introduced a clothing allowance for Fifth Formers and above, which enabled them to buy clothes outwith the Village or, if they wanted, buy priced articles at the Drapery Store. But however they used the allowance, it was up to them to make it last and budget accordingly. A hairdressing allowance was introduced for the girls so that they could go into Bridge of Weir if they wanted rather than standing in line with dozens of others for the free cuts given by a visiting hairdresser who regularly came to the village. And instead of a small amount of pocket money supplemented by "free issues" of so many sweets or so many comics per week for each child, the amount of pocket money was increased to enable the children to make the choices themselves.

The children were given a voice to express their needs and wishes. Years before the National Children's Bureau launched their 'Who Cares?' campaign in 1975 when they produced a book written by children in care about what it was like to be in care, Quarrier's Homes were listening to their children. In 1967 Mr. Mortimer held the first meeting of the Boys' and Girls' Council at which children from all the cottages discussed questions and suggestions about village life from their point of view. The Council still meets regularly and at the meeting in February, 1984, they discussed the question affecting both staff and children: what is the future of Quarrier's Homes?

But there are at least two people today who feel strongly that the most important change for the better at the Homes was neither clothing allowance nor the Council but the introduction of alternatives to the cottage for older children as part of the gradual progression towards independent living outside the Homes. Many hundreds of old boys and girls who lived at Bridge of Weir in the days when you were more or less turned loose and abandoned to the big wide world once your time was up, would sympathise with the sentiments of Catharine Hopkins and David Wilson. Catharine still remembers the nightmare of the day she left Quarrier's in 1920 — the day after she had been informed by the Matron that she was leaving. She had never been out of the Homes on her own before; yet she was taken to Bridge of Weir station and simply told to get the train to Glasgow. She was seventeen, and she didn't even know where Glasgow was. And so she sat in the train and cried all the way, ignored by all the other passengers.

David Wilson at least had the advantage of having made a trial journey on his own into Glasgow before he left the Homes in 1956; but he describes that practice day as "the most traumatic experience I had":

When the great day arrived, I was terrified. I got the bus to Bridge of Weir station. The first train was for Glasgow, but by the time it arrived at Paisley I had had enough. Off I got and as I stood outside the station, thinking, "What shall I do?", the first place I saw was a cinema. In I went. The movie was *Carousel,* my very first movie. Afterwards, straight home — boy, was I glad!

Children in the past were simply not prepared for the shock of leaving the cottage and the shelter of this isolated, enclosed

131

community, and although in the old days they were far better able to look after themselves physically (they could cook, clean, sew), for many the discovery of all the complications and unfamiliarities of the outside world was tremendously hard. They knew nothing of the ways of the world, they had had no training in the use of money, and there had been no intermediate stage to soften the blow between cottage life, lived wholly inside the village, and life outside. All that is now changed. In 1970 one of the cottages in the village was converted into a hostel for older boys and girls where they could live a little more independently, though under supervision, rather than being looked after by cottage parents. The following year, as part of the Centenary celebrations of the founding of the first Home in Glasgow, Quarrier's Old Girls and Boys Club donated the cost of an extension to the cottage and the hostel now has 15 beds for girls and boys of 15 and over. They take turns to cook for each other for a week, are given a budget and have to stick to it. The next stage from the supervised hostel is the unsupervised bed-sit unit where the half-dozen boys and girls are on their own to do their own cooking, buying of food and looking after themselves By this time they might have a job outside the village so they will still be in contact with the Homes and their familiar environment for support and help, but will gradually be spreading their wings. The last stage in this path to independence is one of Quarrier's five flats in nearby Foxbar, Paisley, which the Homes sub-let to their teenagers when they are ready to move out of the village.

Quarrier's Homes have a good reputation for this kind of care of teenagers and it is an area in which they have led the way for other residential homes, both statutory and voluntary. After more than a century William Quarrier would have applauded the fact that his Homes were still pioneering new and imaginative ways of caring for children.

Viscount Muirshiel at the opening of Parklands, the new residential unit at the Epilepsy Centre, in September, 1984

The Centenary Hostel

H.R.H. Prince Charles visiting the Epilepsy Centre during the "Year of the Disabled", July 1981

The Centre Workshop

CHAPTER ELEVEN

Colony to Community

WILLIAM QUARRIER did not live to see the fruition of his last great pioneering work for Scotland, his Colony for Epileptics, now called the Epilepsy Centre. During the 1970s, when things were very much on the move in the children's Homes, there were also great changes occurring at the Centre. The Epilepsy Centre, for some reason, has been cast as the Cinderella in the story of Quarrier's Homes, its features always swamped by the sea of smiling children's faces which the Scottish public has associated with the Homes for over a century. And yet the group of buildings just a few hundred yards further along the road past the Homes always has been, and still is today, the only place in Scotland exclusively for the care and treatment of people with epilepsy; the Centre, as it is known throughout the village, is a national resource and in two years it will celebrate 80 years of pioneering work in the field.

Epilepsy affects perhaps five people out of every 1,000 people in Britain. Great medical advances have taken place in the treatment of the condition during this century. Doctors can isolate two main causes for the seizures, or fits, which someone with epilepsy will have: a genetic, inherited tendency to have attacks because of high brain sensitivity, and brain damage, perhaps through an accident or an illness, like encephalitis. But the why and wherefore of the actual seizures — why they happen when they do — are still shrouded in mystery. There are several different kinds of seizure, and as many

T.V.   K catalysts as there are different people with different personalities and psychological make-ups.

Most people with epilepsy are able to live normal lives in the ordinary community and do a steady job with the help of anti-epileptic drugs and support from their GPs, hospital and social work department. But there are some who have severe difficulties with their epilepsy, ranging from attacks that cannot be sufficiently controlled by drugs to physical and psychological problems which are compounded and exacerbated by their seizures.

Since the early 1970s many changes have taken place at the Centre. Although today the majority of residents are still long-term — men and women who may have been there for twenty years or more and will probably spend the rest of their lives there — the policy of the Centre now is to move in the direction of short-term treatment of people with specific problems with their epilepsy, and the rehabilitation of others towards a return to the outside world. For those who are unable to live a happy and fruitful life in the outside world, rehabilitation aims to achieve a much greater degree of independence within the sheltered community which the Centre provides.

There are seven residential units and cottages for men and women (supervised by housekeeper-type staff), an assessment unit (staffed by nurses), and a training flat and cottages where residents live in varying degrees of independence. In all, the Centre has accommodation for 130 adults and a small group of boys who live in a cottage in the village. Nearly 80 years ago there was only one home for 30 men which was opened in 1906, two years after Quarrier's death. The charge at that time was ten shillings and sixpence a week which, for most colonists, as they were then called, was paid by friends and relatives or the Parish Council. Today the social work departments and, since November 1983, the DHSS pay for each resident.

Those 30 men in the very first home could expect virtually nothing in the way of medical treatment; it was still some years before anti-convulsant drugs began to appear. Before that the treatment consisted of plenty of fresh air, light work and exercise. Staff and colonists mixed and played together, and the Colony often fielded cricket and football team in matches against various outside groups.

The single building was soon joined by others. Another house, this time for women, was built in 1909 and a third for boys and men two years later. In 1933 a fourth building was added with some bed space although the main accommodation was to be for dining room and kitchen. A workshop was built originally as a place indoors where the men could do their carpentry and shoemaking when it was wet, but soon occupational therapy was begun and the colonists did basket-work and weaving, displaying and selling their wares to thousands of visitors to the Homes every year.

It was in the 1930s that important advances were made in the field of recording electrical impulses of the brain. After the war, machines began to appear in hosptals which could scan and record the brain's impulses, thus making it possible to detect any abnormality in the pattern which might be due to epilepsy. The Centre got its first EEG machine (electroencephalograph) in 1948, and as well as using it for their own residents, the medical staff also treated many outpatients from Glasgow hospitals. Nowadays EEGs are much more sophisticated and none more so than the present machine at the Centre; it is the most up-to-date model of the new Medilog 900 ambulatory EEG, an aptly grand title for a marvellous piece of technology which allows the patient to walk around while being recorded instead of having to lie down on a bed, and records on a visual tape for up to 24 hours — 23½ hours longer than the time limit of the conventional EEG.

No new building was done at the Centre after the fourth house was added in 1933 and during the 1940s and 1950s things became rather cramped, with more admissions all the time but no more beds. So several cottages in the children's village were turned into small epilepsy units, mostly for boys. Life went on very much in the same way for the men and women at the Centre; they worked all day in the workshop or the gardens or the kitchens, they retired to their houses at night. The great majority had been doing this for many years and there seemed no sign that they would ever be doing anything else. For the Centre had, like the Homes during the first half of the century, become entrenched; there were increasing numbers of people not just with epilepsy but with other handicaps, such as brain damage and

Hunter House

physical impediments; with a growing army of medical staff watching over them night and day there was inevitably something of the hospitalized institution about the place, symbolised by the big iron gates at the entrance to the main drive which were closed each night. By the 1960s it was clear that the Centre needed change and a move into the future.

A start was made when the first building to be erected for over 30 years was opened in 1969. This was a 24-bedded, modern furnished unit, pleasant and spacious, called Hunter House, after Isabella Hunter, Quarrier's wife. The new unit was designed to be an assessment centre for the residents and a place to which short-term patients could be admitted.

But the real moves towards de-institutionalisation and the creation of a more pleasant, normal community for the men and women at the Centre (who were, after all, not incapable patients but ordinary people with a specific incapacity) were made in the 1970s. Dr. James Minto took over as General Director from Dr. Romanes Davidson in 1974 with specific instructions from the Board of Management to concern himself with the Epilepsy Centre. And so history repeated itself as Dr. Minto followed in the footsteps of the founder and made a pilgrimage south of the Border to see what was being done in the field of epilepsy in England. He went to the first place that William Quarrier had visited at the turn of the century, the Chalfont Colony in Buckinghamshire. There he found sweeping changes in progress.

For many years there had been increasing criticism in England of the old Colonies from social workers, local authorities and public officials on the grounds that they were out-dated, institutionalised and, in some cases, did not provide very good living conditions for their patients. The old Colonies responded to the calls for radical reform. At Chalfont Dr. Minto found that the pot had been thoroughly stirred and many new ingredients added. Most obviously, the name had changed; Chalfont was no longer a Colony, but a Centre for Epilepsy and the colonists not colonists, but residents. And behind the new image were new ideas and policies. The Centre was being run by a very energetic and forward-looking expert on epilepsy, a Scot from Edinburgh, Dr. John Laidlaw, who with his wife Mary, a trained nurse, was working towards rehabilitation into the outside world of any residents who were able, and had begun to admit short-term residents. And a Special Centre for Epilepsy had been opened at Chalfont in association with the National Hospital in London which provided expert medical, assessment and rehabilitative care for short-term admissions of people with problems with their epilepsy.

Dr. Minto came back from Chalfont with many ideas and plans for improving the quality of life for the residents and staff at the re-named Centre in the Homes, and for the direction that the Centre should take in the care and treatment of epilepsy. The building of new, modern living units was high on his list of priorities, but to do this he had to borrow money from the Children's Homes account; the Centre had always been the poor relative as far as donations and legacies were concerned, the lion's share of the contributions always being donated specifically for the children's work. The money required for the Centre was accordingly borrowed and two brand-new units were built— Kelly House and Davidson House, named after the former Chairman and former General Director — each with 12 beds

137

for long-term female residents. They are beautiful units, homely and pleasant, plushly carpeted and comfortably furnished. The women's bedrooms — 5 doubles and 2 singles — are cosy and bright, each decorated with personal ornaments, pictures and mementoes. Nothing could be further from the cold formality of the old-fashioned dormitories in the original Victorian units. Over the next few years the older units were refurbished and modernised and proper names were substituted for the unimaginative numbers; instead of Homes 1, 2 and 3 they became 'Parklands', 'Woodside' and 'Lawview'.

The next area for consideration was the work available at the Centre. At that time all the residents were engaged either in gardening or the workshop. The workshop took on light industrial contract work for neighbouring firms and paid residents a small amount of money each month. The work involved things like counting out small components and sealing them in containers, punching holes in various components or assembling free film envelopes; for those residents with a degree of brain damage or some other handicap besides their epilepsy, this work was simple and agreeable; but for others it was boring and provided no mental stimulus or challenge to their abilities. So a new Craft Centre was opened where some of the more able residents could work with metal and wood and other materials, constructing and finishing a whole range of goods from chairs to salt cellars and hanging baskets, all of which went on sale to visitors. The Craft Centre has flourished over the years and a cottage in the village was opened in May, 1984, which sells its wares along with many other arts and crafts.

For the first time in its history the Epilepsy Centre got a full-time Leisure Officer whose job it was to provide outings, activities and interesting clubs for the residents which would give them something more to look forward to in the evenings than the communal television. The present Leisure Officer organises a huge variety of activities for the residents, from a keep-fit class and regular video shows to outings to the Burrell Collection and indoor football at the Sports Centre in the village.

Following the example of Chalfont, the Centre began to move towards assisting those who were able to live in the outside community and some did leave and stay in hostels in Glasgow and Edinburgh run by the Church of Scotland. To prepare residents for the move, a Rehabilitation Officer was appointed for the first time.

That was in 1978; and at Easter, 1979, Dr. Minto welcomed as the new Chief Consultant of the Centre Dr. John Laidlaw who had done so much at Chalfont. In the years since then, Dr. Laidlaw has been steering the Centre into a position where it is now providing a wide range of care and treatment for epilepsy. There is a large population of men and women there now who have been at the Centre for much of their lives and would not be able to survive outside; so although the current fashion in all kinds of care is to help the person in the 'real' outside community, Dr. Laidlaw and his staff will continue to provide long-term care for those people who can enjoy a far better quality of life within the sheltered and supportive framework of the Centre. For many, the Centre is their home where they have friends and steady work and they are part of a community which tries to be as normal and unhospitalised as possible. To this end, Dr. Laidlaw made radical changes in the staffing of the Centre soon after his arrival, substituting housekeeper-type staff (Caring Staff) in the residential units for nursing staff in an attempt to normalise the environment and help the residents feel less like patients. Dr. Laidlaw also substantially reduced and controlled the number of drugs which many residents were prescribed. Anti-convulsant drugs are very powerful indeed and many residents had been prescribed several different kinds in an attempt to control their fits. In some cases this had resulted in intoxication. Dr. Laidlaw's policy is that it is better that residents occasionally have fits and are otherwise healthy than that they have too many drugs which may mean fewer fits but would leave them lethargic and slow and unable to enjoy life.

The other arm of the Centre's work which has developed rapidly since 1979 is that of short-term admissions. Hunter House, plus three cottages in the village and a training flat in the Centre, now form the Assessment and Rehabilitation Unit, rather like the Special Centre at Chalfont. People are admitted to the Unit if the Centre feels it can do something for them within a limited period of time. The treatment might be the reduction of the amount and number of anti-epileptic drugs someone is taking; it might be to determine whether in fact the fits *are* epileptic or due to some other cause; or it could involve helping to rehabilitate someone whose epilepsy has caused severe behavioural and psychological problems with which they cannot cope. The Rehabilitation team is led by Mrs. Mary Laidlaw and their concern is not simply to teach practical skills like cooking or managing money or what to do about collecting social security payments — all things that someone preparing to leave the Centre would need to be able to do; they feel that another very important arm of rehabilitation is to help people come to terms with their epilepsy by concerning itself with the mental and emotional attitudes of someone with epilepsy, by helping the person to live with all the complications and distresses which the condition causes, and by building up their confidence and self-image which the indignity and irrationality of seizures can so easily shatter.

The Centre is still very much in the process of change, with new developments and plans afoot all the time. There is now an Adult Education Unit which provides remedial teaching — a very important addition since some residents have a degree of mental retardation on top of their epilepsy which gives them learning difficulties and others have been deprived of a proper education in the past because of constant seizures. To relieve the boredom of the workshop for the more able residents, other activities such as music and painting clubs have been started and there are plans to set up a sheltered workshop in the Centre, employing the residents in some more demanding work like printing or bookbinding.

Dr. Laidlaw has done a great deal to stimulate informed interest, both medical and lay, in epilepsy and its problems. He is co-author of the only British textbook on epilepsy to be published this century, *A Textbook of Epilepsy;* and together, Dr. Laidlaw and Mrs. Laidlaw have written *Epilepsy Explained,* a very readable book for the ordinary person. They are currently putting the finishing touches to another book, *People with Epilepsy: How can we help them?* The Centre aims to continue to be the major pioneer, educator and publiciser of the care and treatment of epilepsy throughout Scotland. Within its own four walls the changes at the Centre over the last decade have, most importantly of all, affected directly the quality of life for the individuals who live and work there: for a couple like George and Martie Bowie, for instance, who have been in the Centre for over 15 years but who have, for the last three years lived in a cottage in the Homes. Neither could have imagined, even 5 years ago, when they were living up at the Centre, looked after by nurses and doing very little for themselves that one day they would be cooking, shopping and managing for themselves, living independently and on the road, perhaps, to complete independence and a new life outside the village.

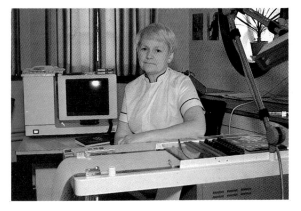

The new E.E.G. machine at the Centre

CHAPTER TWELVE

Crisis

FAR AWAY IN the north-east corner of India the town of Kalimpong looks out towards Tibet across the snow-covered peaks of the Himalayas. There, in 1900, Dr. John Graham, a Church of Scotland missionary, founded a community of cottage Homes for the hundreds of poor and abandoned Anglo-Indian children he saw every day in the tea plantations he visited on his missionary travels through the country.

Dr. Graham's Homes in Kalimpong are part of the Quarrier's Homes story, past and present. The Doctor had modelled the entire complex, right down to the design of the cottages, on Quarrier's children's village which he had visited at the end of the 1890s. And Dr. James Minto, who joined Quarrier's Homes as General Director and successor to Dr. Romanes Davidson in 1974, had been principal of the Kalimpong Homes from 1958 to 1971.

Dr. Minto took up his new post at a time when change was in the air; and in the last few years he has had to guide the Homes through a major crisis which has forced them to rethink and reorganise their work completely. There were hundreds of children living in the village when Dr. Minto came, but since 1980 the numbers have shrunk to less than 100 and the forecast is that by 1986 there will be only 21 children in two or three cottages, with 26 older teenagers living in the hostel and bedsit units. Since 1981, to ensure the survival of the Homes without their traditional large numbers of children, Dr. Minto has had to channel the resources and expertise of the organisation into other areas of care, a process which is still going on.

What happened in the ten short years since 1974 when Dr. Minto spoke at his inaugural Annual General Meeting of the "winds of change" which were beginning to blow around the Homes? A gradual change in the relationship between the Homes and the local authorities was becoming evident at that time. During the 1960s Quarrier's had been financially secure and more or less independent, but by the 1970s they were more and more reliant upon the maintenance grants that came with each child referred to the Homes by the local authority. It became clear to Dr. Minto that in future Quarrier's would have to work much more closely with the statutory authorities and fall in with their ideas and plans for the care of children.

These plans did not favour the set-up at Bridge of Weir. As late as the 1960s this model village in pleasant surroundings deep in the Renfrewshire countryside where 500 children lived, worked and played was still acceptable to current child care theories. But by the 1970s, after the new social work departments had been formed with wide-ranging powers to help the child in its natural family, this kind of residential care was coming to be regarded as old-fashioned. Local authorities did not approve of an isolated complex of cottages where the children led a life usually far removed from the kind of life and circumstances they came from and would return to; social workers looked with suspicion on a self-contained community from which the children seldom ventured, even to go to school: until 1980, when the boys and girls were enrolled at many different schools in the Port Glasgow and Greenock area, all the children were educated at their very own William Quarrier School within the Homes grounds. This sort of residential care now found itself out of step with current fashions in child care which stressed helping children in their homes or in small, specialist units.

Dr. Minto held disscussions with the local authorities and soon realised that the way forward for the Homes was joint projects outwith the village complex. The Homes already had three outposts, small residential Children's Homes outside the village. These were 'Overbridge' in Glasgow, 'Merton' Home in Largs and another small residential home in Girvan called 'Seabank' where some of the more educationally gifted children from Bridge of Weir were transferred and enrolled in schools in the neighbourhood. These were children with the potential to sit Highers and continue with further education. Now came two entirely new projects outside the village, conceived, funded and carried out jointly with the local authorities: an Intermediate Treatment Centre and a residential unit for disturbed and maladjusted children (technically called a List G School).

The IT Centre at West Yonderton (near Glasgow Airport) was begun in 1975 and was a continuation of pioneering work started at Turnberry as far back as 1966. Working both on a farm at West Yonderton and in community centres in the children's home town, the social workers help youngsters and teenagers with all kinds of problems: perhaps they have just come out of a List D School, or they may be glue-sniffers, or they may be school "refusers". The IT team deals with about 85 children each week who come regularly for up to six months; through group work, discussion and continuous liaison with local social workers, the team at West Yonderton try to help the youngsters over their difficulties.

The List G residential unit for maladjusted and disturbed young-sters was opened at Southannan in Fairlie, near Largs, in 1978 — the first of its kind in Scotland. The children there, mostly aged 12 and over, have severe behavioural and emotional problems and the aim of the team of social workers, teachers and caring staff is to rehabilitate them to the point where they can live peaceably and responsibly once more in the ordinary community. It is a very long process which involves building up trusting and dependable relationships with the children, many of whom come to Southannan with a very poor self-image and an unhappy, unstable family background.

Both West Yonderton and Southannan are well in the forefront of child care in Scotland and have gradually developed into highly professional units especially since 1979 when Mr. Michael Laxton was seconded from the Scottish Office at the request of Quarrier's Homes to be their Development Adviser; among other things his duties included the overseeing of the work at West Yonderton and Southannan, and since then the two schemes have become very

Southannan

successful. Southannan even merited a mention in *Home or Away?*, Strathclyde Social Work Department's recent report on residential care strategy for the future: it was singled out as an example of the very good work undertaken by some voluntary child care organisations.

Strathclyde Region was born on May 16, 1975; it was a very important day for Quarrier's Homes because the creation (under the 1973 Local Government (Scotland) Act) of this huge new regional authority, stretching from Skye to the Clyde and from Renfrewshire to Lanarkshire and comprising 22 former local authorities, was to have a direct effect on the numbers of children in the village. With its enormous budget, extensive powers and well-defined policies the social work department of the new region made its presence felt immediately in the area of child care. Its policies were clear: as had been the trend of child care for some years now, first and foremost children were to be kept in their own homes and helped within the community if at all possible. Community care was the ideal to be achieved. What this involved was discussed in a report by the Officer/ Member group of the region's social work committee; entitled *Room to Grow* (1978), it defined community care as follows:

> Any action, initiative, provision or policy which enables children to remain with their families in their own community

The new region had the money to finance the many back-up social services which community care requires, like nursery schools, play groups and day-care centres where working mothers can leave their children. Social work departments can also work closely with, for example, housing departments to help avoid the accumulation of rent-arrears which so often in the past resulted in eviction and the children having to come into care. Or, as the Report suggested, the Region could develop a scheme by which a number of peripatetic houseparents could temporarily look after children in their own home if, for example, the mother was in hospital — another common reason for children being placed in care.

However, if a child had to be taken from or could not live with his natural parents, Strathclyde advocated fostering or adoption as the next best thing. Accordingly, very soon after its creation the Region launched a massive fostering campaign and tried to get as many children out of residential care as possible. They wanted everyone to be in on it, statutory Homes as well as voluntaries, and Quarrier's Homes were quick to respond. In 1977 they embarked upon the Quarrier's Family Fostering Project, a joint scheme in which they worked very closely with Strathclyde social workers and successfully fostered about 50 of their children, many of whom had been in the Homes for years.

Since then Quarrier's Homes have fostered more than 100 boys and girls and at the moment there are still a number of children in the process of finding homes. Strathclyde firmly believes that *every* child in care should have the opportunity to be fostered and Quarrier's are equally anxious that their children should not remain in the Homes a moment longer than is necessary. But fostering is a very delicate and difficult operation which demands careful planning, scrupulous assessment of child and foster family and a lot of time. It's like grafting skin from one body to another. There has been a great deal of fostering in Strathclyde over the last few years and Quarrier's have had the sad experience of seeing some of their children fostered too quickly and not carefully enough. Their clinical psychologist has then to put the pieces together again when a fostering breaks down and a child is returned to the Homes upset and depressed. And for some of the children who have lived in their cottages for years and years and have come to regard them as home, and who are suddenly told that they are to be fostered, it can be a distressing experience. It is a heartbreaking situation, not just for the child but for the cottage parents who have looked after the child like their own.

If fostering is not possible and a child has to come into care Strathclyde's policy has been to use residential care, but during the 1970s they began to use their own Homes more and more in preference to the voluntary Homes. All these factors, plus the dramatic drop in the birthrate from the late 1960s onwards, were reflected in the decreasing numbers of children in Quarrier's Homes. There were nearly 500 children when Dr. Minto came in 1974, of whom about 75 were babies and toddlers. There are no babies and toddlers there today. In 1978, the Centenary Year of the establishment of the Homes at Bridge of Weir, there were still nearly 400 children although Dr. Minto referred in his annual report to expert opinion in child care which predicted that there would never again be the same numbers of children in residential care. However Quarrier's did not seem unduly worried; they felt quite secure in the knowledge that their cottages were full and so far the decrease in numbers had been slow and steady.

But suddenly the unthinkable happened. One moment, at the beginning of 1980, Quarrier's were looking after more than 300 children; in the next, by December, 1980, only three months into the new financial year, they had 50 fewer children than they needed to cover their costs and Strathclyde Region was informing them that the numbers would not be made up. Quarrier's Homes were facing a crisis.

How had it happened? In the long term the Region's policies and the fall in the birth rate had taken their toll of the numbers, but the sudden and dramatic drop in admissions was a result of something quite different: Strathclyde had been putting its own house in order. A computer was installed in their headquarters in 1980 which rationalised the whole network of Homes and the number of places available in the Region, and Strathclyde discovered that they could accommodate far more children in their own Homes than they had been doing. And at a time when they were closing some of their own Homes because of falling numbers and financial stringency they were naturally anxious not to fill up voluntary places at the expense of their own.

Quarrier's can hardly be blamed for being caught short, because the decrease was so sudden. At a meeting with Strathclyde officials as late as June, 1980, just six months before the blow fell, the Region had not made it clear that the numbers they would be referring for the next financial year would not be enough to cover Quarrier's costs. On the other hand, all that Strathclyde was really doing was forcing the pace, dealing the blow quickly which was to come anyway. For years and years Quarrier's had been out on a limb in terms of residential child care in Scotland, still providing for hundreds of children at a time when all other Homes were for small groups; still improving and expanding the village complex — a new Sports Centre was added in 1977 — many years after similar large voluntary organisations like Barnardo's Homes in Barkingside and Aberlour Children's Homes* in Banffshire had run down their villages and diversified into smaller children's Homes and specialist units all over the country. The time to change was the late 1960s and early 1970s as Barnardo's and Aberlour Homes had done, at a time when Quarrier's had plenty of money and could have ploughed it into areas of specialist care, smaller satellite Homes, care for the mentally handicapped, the elderly or any other groups that the local authorities could not cope with. But Quarrier's Homes missed the boat.

In a way, though, even if the Homes had been more aware, like Barnardo's and Aberlour, of the changing climate of child care, even if they had been far-sighted enough to see the day when there would

*Now the *"Aberlour Child Care Trust"* with headquarters in Stirling.

Respite Care Unit

Some Abbeyfield residents with the Quarrier's village minister, Rev. Montgomerie and Mrs. Montgomerie

Dr. Minto, the General Director

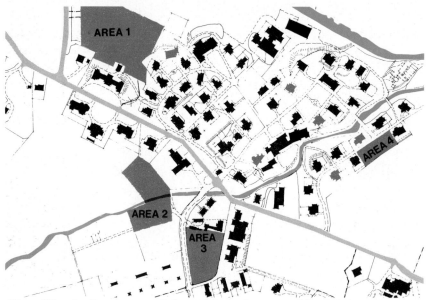

Plan of Housing Development (9.8 acres) for both commercial and sheltered housing.

no longer be the need for their huge residential complex, and had decided that the village should be run down, that awareness would not have been much use. For the Homes' best qualities and most enduring traditions would have been their worst enemies. Running down the village and looking positively into different kinds of care for the future would have meant saying to the local authorities: "We will take no more children"; Quarrier's Homes, with its cherished tradition of helping any child in need, would never have done that and did not do so during the 1970s, either. It might have meant, as it did for Barnardo's and Aberlour, adopting a more business-like and professional attitude to money by advertising for funds and support for new ventures — and this, too, the traditions of the Homes would not have allowed. Quarrier's Homes have never made a public appeal for money.

Instead, they carried on as usual. It was all too easy to assume that all would be well since their admission rates throughout the 1970s were steady and their cottages in use were full. The local authorities were using the Homes as they needed them and it was all too easy to believe that this would continue indefinitely. When Strathclyde discovered all of a sudden that they no longer needed these places, the effect on Quarrier's was devastating. At a crisis board meeting in December, 1980, the cold facts were: 50 vacancies, 50 local authority maintenance grants to be deducted from income, a resultant overdraft of £250,000, the prospect of a working loss for the year of £400,000 and the imminent closure of cottages and redundancy of large numbers of staff. In all, nearly 100 cottage parents and other staff had to be made redundant over the next three years, children were moved from one cottage and merged with another and 5 cottages had to be closed.

By the time the next board meeting came round in March, 1981, Dr. Minto had been informed by the local authorities that the Homes would never again receive the same numbers of children. It was clear that Quarrier's Homes could no longer be the organisation it had been; caring for children could no longer be their life's work as it had been for more than a hundred years.

CHAPTER THIRTEEN

Resolution

COULD QUARRIER'S HOMES now survive and, if so, how? In the worrying early months of 1981, as cottages closed and staff were made redundant, this was the question facing Dr. Minto and the Board of Management. The grim situation confronting them — rapidly decreasing numbers of children and financial collapse — demanded positive and radical action. Somehow they had to re-organise Quarrier's Homes without children into a useful, viable voluntary agency with something to offer Scotland in the 1980s.

Quarrier's rose to the challenge. In June, 1982, Dr. Minto presented his **8 Year Plan** to the Board — as bold, imaginative and daunting a scheme as anything William Quarrier himself ever devised. The **8 Year Plan** was an attempt to create a completely new community, to change Quarrier's Homes into Quarrier's Village, a community where needy groups like the elderly and the mentally handicapped can be supported and helped, but in an environment which is as normal as possible. Instead of filling the empty cottages exclusively with all kinds of dependent groups and ending up with a village-sized Emergency Ward 10 in the middle of the Renfrewshire countryside, Quarrier's tried to achieve a balance by introducing, also, several small industries and businesses into vacant buildings, by acting as landlord to various organisations and, most ambitiously of all, negotiating the sale of small tracts of land and several cottages to a commercial housing developer. This part of the plan will bring in much-needed revenue to the Homes which have to maintain a very large complex of cottages and amenities.

Dr. Minto's **8 Year Plan** had already been partially in operation for a year before he presented the formal package to the Board in 1982. 1990 may seem a long way off, and Quarrier's Village is still very much in the throes of change, but the four phases of development which the Plan isolated are well advanced.

Phase 1 deals with the future of Quarrier's with fewer children and the groups which will replace them as numbers dwindle. At present (April, 1984) there are about 90 children still living in cottages and another 22 in bedsit and hostel units. The majority of these children are 12 years of age and older and many have been in the Homes for years. Quarrier's are determined to see them through to independence if foster parents cannot be found for them, if they don't want to be fostered, or if they cannot return to their own families so there will still be children in the village until the last of these boys and girls has passed through the hostel and bedsits. For the future there is still a faint chance that children will continue to come to Quarrier's; at the time of writing, Strathclyde Region is considering whether to maintain about 50 places in the Homes for children in the 12 and over age group who would live in one or two cottages and the hostel and bedsit units. The situation is still very uncertain, though, and Strathclyde has made no promises.

In the village children's places are being taken by other people who need the support and help which Quarrier's have provided for over 110 years. Campbell Maltman Home, which used to be full of toddlers and babies, is now the Respite Care Unit for severely and profoundly handicapped children and young adults. The aim of this highly professional and energetic unit is to provide short-term care for the handicapped in order to give their families and parents some relief and support. But beds are also available for emergencies if, for example, the mother of a handicapped child has to go to hospital suddenly and the family cannot cope. The Unit has about 125 families on its books. People come for varying lengths of time, perhaps from Monday to Friday or over the weekend, and with varying frequency— once a month, every two months or just twice a year. The Respite

Care Unit is an extremely valuable resource which provides expert care in an area of need which is very great today.

Another urgent problem which local authorities need help in tackling is that of getting mentally handicapped people out of hospitalised institutions in which some of them have spent most of their lives. Quarrier's are doing marvellous work in three cottages in the village which have been turned into hostels for residents from Lennox Castle, a hospital for the mentally ill near the Campsie Hills north of Glasgow. The project is funded by the Greater Glasgow Health Board, while the cottages are staffed and run by Quarrier's Homes. The cottages have given a chance for a new life to many who have spent the last twenty years in a bed in a hospital ward, and the scheme has been so successful that Argyll and Clyde Health Board plan to send patients from their hospitals to another cottage which will open in the village. In addition, Quarrier's small Home in Girvan, 'Seabank', has been converted into a hostel for those who will eventually be able to leave the shelter of the village cottages and there are plans to open another hostel in Paisley which Quarrier will rent from the Aberlour Child Care Trust (formerly Aberlour Children's Homes).

Quarrier's have also given accommodation within their cottages to the elderly. An Abbeyfield 'Quarrier's' Society has been formed, chaired by the Homes' Rev. Robert Montgomery, and two cottages in the village are now in use. Abbeyfield is a national charitable organisation which provides sheltered accommodation for elderly men and women, not in a group of flats but under one roof in a large house. The residents each have their own bed-sitting room and are able to live quite privately from the rest of the household if they wish, but they receive two hot meals a day and there is always a housekeeper on hand for help and support. Morton-Perry Home, built during the First World War as a cottage for the children of soldiers, is now home for six men and women, and Campbell-Snowdon Home has been converted into a Extra-Care Abbeyfield Unit. This is for residents who need a bit of extra looking after in things like dressing, feeding, toilet, etc., but are by no means bed-ridden.

It's a lovely spot to come and live in and the new Abbeyfield residents appreciate the pleasant surroundings, the quiet traffic-free avenues and the easy access to Bridge of Weir by means of a half-hourly bus service which leaves from inside the grounds. Quarrier's have a lot to offer the elderly and more accommodation for them is on the way; several cottages are due to be converted into sheltered housing there will be two more houses on the lines of the Abbeyfield ones, and down in Largs the 'Merton' Home has been converted into an old people's home.

Quarrier's are acting as landlords to many other groups. One of the cottages is now used by KIND (Kids In Need and Distress), a Liverpool-based voluntary organisation which gives deprived children and their families from the city a week's holiday in the country. Many of the children who come to the village have never had a holiday before, and as well as joining in the village life they participate in lots of open-air activities organised by KIND, from sailing and canoeing to rock-climbing.

Women's Aid have the use of one cottage, and another houses the Intermediate Treatment Resource Centre for Scotland. Scottish Industries Training and Management Services, in conjunction with the Manpower Services Commission and Quarrier's Village, run 10-day residential courses in leadership for young people during the year and have a cottage in the village.

Of course the biggest danger in filling up the empty cottages with so many different groups of people is that the village becomes a peculiar and uneasy hotch-potch of minorities, not a community but just a collection of buildings. Phases 2 and 3 of the **8 Year Plan** are an attempt to avoid this disintegration. In April 1984 agreement was reached between Quarrier's and Barratt Urban Renewal (Scotland) Ltd., and Barratt (Glasgow) Ltd, a major housing developer, for Barratt to develop and build on 11 acres of land all around the village and convert four cottages in the village into sheltered houses. Dr. Minto believes that many people will jump at the chance to own their own house in such pleasant countryside within comfortable commuting distance of Glasgow and that this framework of private housing, as well as bringing in much-needed revenue for Quarrier's, will give the village more of the feel of an ordinary community. But

153

it is not enough simply to surround the village with a new housing estate. Dr. Minto recognises that there should be development from within, too; this will be done by putting ten or twelve former children's cottages on the open market so that ordinary men and women and their families can come and live in the very heart of this extraordinary community.

The greatest challenge and most difficult goal to achieve is the third phase of the Plan; the integration of all the elderly people, the mentally handicapped adults, the charitable organisations, the private householders, the remaining children, the Epilepsy Centre residents and all the other various tenants of the cottages. It looks like an impossible task, but Dr. Minto believes firmly in the vision of a new, integrated Quarrier's Village and is confident that, though it may take many years, eventually the village will settle down and take shape. It already has many village amenities which hundreds of children have used over the years, including a swimming pool, Sports Centre and Park. Then there is the Post Office and a General Store and several small businesses which have recently taken premises within the village: a hairdressing salon, a joiner's, a firm making bedroom and kitchen units and a wholesale toymaker's are just a few of them. Dr. Minto's hope is that all the groups in the village will use the facilities Quarrier's have to offer and that the recent formation of a Village Council, with representatives from every group, will foster good relations and familiarity throughout this disparate community. The Village Church, Mount Zion, also has an important part to play in the life of Quarrier's Village and negotiations are under way to have the Chaplain Rev. Robert Montgomery, become a Community Chaplain, responsible to the Greenock Presbytery.

With the Village as its headquarters, Quarrier's plan to do new work all over Strathclyde and perhaps beyond. The final phase of the **8 Year Plan** is a natural development of some of the work outside the Village started in the 1970s. It would complicate an already difficult situation in the Village to introduce any more needy groups there, so Dr. Minto and the Board plan that any future innovative, progressive projects and specialist units will be *outside* the confines of the Village. At the moment Quarrier's are negotiating with Central Region's Social

Work Department to open another IT Centre on the West Yonderton model and an Alternative Education Unit on the lines of Southannan; Aberlour Child Care Trust is also involved with Quarrier's in planning these two projects. Also on the cards is a Family Centre in Greenock which Quarrier's are planning with the Local Authority.

In the future Quarrier's Village plans to work closely with other local authorities and voluntary organisations in areas like the care of the under-fives in their community, the care of adolescents, glue-sniffing and alcoholism in young people, looking after the elderly and mentally handicapped, and many other urgent social problems of today.

Margaret Rowntree has come back to Quarrier's Village. Forty-five years after she left the Orphan Homes of Scotland as a young girl of 18, she has returned to live in cottage 43, the Abbeyfield house for elderly men and women. She was admitted to the Orphan Homes in 1927 as a little girl of 6 after her mother died. Her first memory is of standing outside cottage 15 (now used by the Epilepsy Centre) and catching sight of the grand lead-framed stained glass panel above the front door; she had come by train from the City Home that morning and had no idea where she was, but she knew this wasn't her mother's house and she was afraid to go in. Margaret's half-brother had also come to Bridge of Weir and stayed in the same cottage for the first night; but after that he was taken to a boys' cottage and she hardly saw him again for the 12 years she was there, except across the playground fence at school and sometimes when his cottage marched through the village on their Sunday afternoon walk.

Physically the village has changed little since Margaret left; the grey stone cottages, the tree-lined avenues, the bridge over the Cattie, the Church and the Epilepsy Centre up the road are all more or less as they were. But what a difference Margaret sees in the life of the children there today. She marvels at a life style much nearer the ideal of home than in the hard times of the 1920s and 1930s when she was a girl. Walking round Quarrier's today she meets boys careering round corners on their bicycles and others strolling along the avenues listening to radios. In every cottage there's an atmosphere of normality and domesticity that greets you like the smell of cooking. In one cottage it's just before Easter everyone is getting excited about parties and Easter eggs; two little girls are sprawled across the living room floor making Easter hats for the Fuzzy Wuzzy Club in the evening; in another it's bathtime and a small damp-haired boy is wandering through the hall in his dressing gown on his way to watch television. Each cottage is different, and Quarrier's try to be flexible and adapt to the special needs of individual children. In one cottage the cottage mother and father have fostered all six children and teenagers who live there; now they work round the clock like ordinary parents looking after a big family instead of sharing responsibility with a team of relief workers. Liz Edwards, the Youth and Community Worker, organises group activities and outings for a number of teenagers who are unsettled in their cottages or have problems with school and need a different kind of care from the traditional cottage set-up. Quarrier's also run their own Youth Training Scheme for the older teenagers in the hostel and bedsit units; at the moment some boys are working in the Epilepsy Craft Centre and in one or two of the new small businesses in the village.

It's all worlds removed from the Orphan Homes of Scotland Margaret remembers, especially now that there are so few children living in the cottages and their places have been taken by all kinds of newcomers. The Village, the new Quarrier's, is still changing and only time will tell if the strange, strong mixture will settle and the **8 Year Plan** prove a realistic, practicable vision or a marvellous pipedream. There are many challenges to face, the greatest of which will be to convince the professional child care world and its social workers that Quarrier's is a highly qualified, forward-looking and dynamic organisation which Scotland cannot do without. They have strong credentials already: great strength and flexibility, proven by the way in which the organisation has changed itself so drastically in such a short time; and 113 years of caring for people behind them. Most of all, Quarrier's still retain the great enthusiasm and energy of their founder; whatever the future holds for the new village, this will be its strength.

Appendices

Appendix I

QUARRIER'S RESPONSIBILITIES — 1984

CARE FOR CHILDREN AND YOUNG PERSONS

Village	Cottages — 7 Units		70
	Hostel & Bed Sits		26
	Special Units		12
Foxbar, Paisley	Flats for Young Persons		6
Overbridge, Glasgow			8
Southannan, Fairlie List G School			24
West Yonderton, Intermediate Treatment Centre			124
		Total	270

CARE FOR HANDICAPPED

Village, Campbell Maltman—Respite Care		130
Fountainview (Mentally Handicapped Adults) (5 units)		40
Seabank, Girvan—Hostel		9
Gallowhill, Paisley—Hostel		9
	Total	188

CARE FOR ELDERLY

Village	Cottages 2 units		18
Merton, Largs			9
		Total	27

CARE FOR ADULTS WITH EPILEPSY

Village	Cottages 5 units		45
	Centre 7 units		85
		Total	130

QUARRIER'S RESPONSIBILITIES—*SUMMARY*

	Village	*Outside Communities*	*Total*
Care for Children, Young Persons	108	162	270
Care for Handicapped	170	18	188
Care for Elderly	18	9	27
Care for Adults with Epilepsy	130	—	130
			615

ADDITIONAL RESPONSIBILITIES FOR:

Swimming Pool	Education Areas	Sports Centre
Post Office	Recreation and Play Areas	Medical Centres
Craft Centre and Shop	Hattrick Farm	Garden Centre
Main Hall	Workshops (Occupational and Industrial Therapy)	

158

QUARRIER'S RESPONSIBILITIES — *ACTING AS LANDLORD* — VILLAGE 1984

CARING UNITS

Abbeyfield Quarrier's Society—2 units—27   Woman's Aid—1 unit

KIND (Kids in Need and Distress) 2 units   SITMS (Residential Training Courses) 1 unit

Boarding House (Young Trainees) 1 unit

BUSINESSES

Barnshake Farm Dairies   Rosemary's Hairdressing and Beauty Salon

Burndale Workshops   Pottery

Dormouse Designs   I.T. Resource Centre

Flair fashions   John Lithgow Publications

Dressmaker   Islay Sportswear

Kennet Electronics

Appendix II

DEPLOYMENT OF BUILDINGS

1 Assistants Residence
2 Woman's Aid Refuge
3 Craft Centre Shop/Flat
4 Family Care

5 Vacant

6 To be Flatted and Sold
7 Family Care
8 Former Boys & Girls Assoc. Hostel
9 Bed/Sit
10 Epilepsy Centre and Rehabilitation Unit
11 Family Care
12 Family Care
13 Epilepsy Centre and Rehabilitation Unit
14 Family Care
15 Epilepsy Centre and Rehabilitation Unit
16a Staff Flat
16b Staff Flat
17 Care of Elderly
18a Family Care Flat
18b Staff Flat
19 Care of Elderly

20 Chaplaincy Centre
21 S.I.T.M.S.
22 Family Care
23 Fountainview (Mentally Handicapped Adults)
24 Fountainview (Mentally Handicapped Adults)
25 To be Flatted and Sold
26 Special Unit (Boys/Epilepsy)
27 Epilepsy Centre Unit
28 Epilepsy Centre and Rehabilitation Unit
29 Fountainview (Mentally Handicapped Adults)
30 Assistants Residence/Flat
31 Staff Residence
32 Hostel
33 Family Care
34 Bed Sit
35 Vacant
36 K.I.N.D. Organisation (Liverpool)
38 Family Care
39 Family Care
40 K.I.N.D. Organisation (Liverpool

41 Private Accommodation
42 Family Care
43 Abbeyfield

CAMPBELL SNOWDON—Abbeyfield/Extra Care

LAING SHREWSBURY—Assistant Residence/I.T. Resource Centre (Scotland)

CAMPBELL MALTMAN—Respite Care Unit

ELISE—S.I.T.M.S.

Bibliography

THE LIFE STORY OF WILLIAM QUARRIER John Urquhart *(R.L.Allan & Son, 1901)*

A ROMANCE OF FAITH Alexander Gammie *(Pickering & Inglis, 1937)*

THE POWER I PLEDGE James Ross *University Press, Glasgow, 1971)*

THE NINETEENTH CENTURY

GLASGOW The Making of a City Andrew Gibb *(Croom Helm, 1983)*

THE NEW STATISTICAL ACCOUNT OF LANARKSHIRE 1841
(William Blackwood & Sons)

THE FORMER AND PRESENT STATE OF GLASGOW
James Clelland *(Bell & Bain, 1837)*

STATISTICAL TABLES RELATIVE TO THE CITY OF GLASGOW
James Clelland *(James Lumsden & Sons, 1823)*

MAINTENANCE OF THE POOR James Clelland *(Glasgow, 1828)*

PICTURES OF PAUPERISM ed. Donald Ross *(George Gallie, 1847)*

THE DAWN OF SCOTTISH SOCIAL WELFARE A Survey from medieval
times to 1863 Thomas Ferguson *(Thomas Nelson & Sons Ltd., 1945)*

THE CHILDREN'S LABOUR QUESTION Reprints from the "Daily News" (1899)

THIS IS YOUR CHILD The Story of the N.S.P.C.C.
Anne Allan & Arthur Morton *(Routledge, Keegan & Paul, 1961)*

**ANNUAL REPORTS OF THE GLASGOW SOCIETY FOR THE
PREVENTION OF CRUELTY TO CHILDREN 1885-1889**

BARNARDO Gillian Wagner *(Eyre & Spottiswoode,1979)*

THE LIFE OF GEORGE MÜLLER William Henry Hardy *(Morgan & Scott, 1914)*

MEMOIRS OF THE LATE Dr. BARNARDO Mrs. Barnardo & James
Marchant *(Hodder & Stoughton, 1907)*

THE HEALTH OF GLASGOW 1818-1925 A. K. Chalmers *(Bell & Bain, 1930)*

CANADA

CANADIANS IN THE MAKING A. Lowe   *(Longman, Canada, 1958)*

THE LITTLE IMMIGRANTS Kenneth Bagnell   *(Macmillan of Canada, 1980)*

BRITISH CHILDREN IN CANADIAN HOMES Ellen Agnes Bilbrough
(Houghton & Co., London, 1879)

EPILEPSY

EPILEPSY EXPLAINED M. V. Laidlaw & John Laidlaw *(Churchill Livingstone, 1980)*

A TEXTBOOK OF EPILEPSY ed. Laidlaw & Riches chapter 15
(Churchill Livingstone, 1982, 2nd revised edition)

THE TWENTIETH CENTURY

THE THIRD STATISTICAL ACCOUNT OF SCOTLAND
Glasgow Volume   *(Collins, 1958)*

CHILDREN IN CARE The development of the service for the deprived child Jean S.
Heywood   *(1978 revised edition)*

THE CHILD'S GENERATION Child Care Policy in Britain Jean Packman
(Basil Blackwell & Martin Robertson, 1981 revised edition)

PAPERS, REPORTS, etc.

THE ADMINISTRATION OF CHILDREN'S HOMES (Scotland)
REGULATIONS 1963   *(HMSO)*

STAFFING OF LOCAL AUTHORITY CHILDREN'S DEPARTMENTS
Report by the Scottish Advisory Council on Child Care 1963   *(HMSO)*

THE CHILD CARE SERVICE AT WORK Report by the Scottish Advisory
Council on Child Care 1963   *(HMSO)*

CHILD CARE 1966 Report by the Secretary of State for Scotland   *(HMSO)*

REPORT OF THE COMMITTEE ON HOMELESS CHILDREN The "Clyde"
Report   *(HMSO, Edinburgh 1946)*

WHOSE CHILDREN? Letter from Marjory Allen of Hurtwood to the "Times"
(July 15, 1944)

ROOM TO GROW Report of a Regional Council officer/member working group on child
care services in Strathclyde   *(1978)*

HOME OR AWAY? Report by the Director on residential child care
(Strathclyde Regional Council Social Work Department, 1983)

MANUSCRIPTS, ANNUAL REPORTS

DIARIES OF ADMISSION 1890-1891   *(Quarrier's Archives)*

NARRATIVES OF FACTS 1872-1983   *(Quarrier's Archives)*

Index

All page numbers set in Italics denote illustrations

162

Index

All page numbers set in Italics denote illustrations

Index

All page numbers set in Italics denote illustrations